Get Up, Get Going

Get Up, Get Going

TALES OF A COUNTRY VETERINARIAN

Dr. A.J. Neumann, D.V.M.
with Renae B. Vander Schaaf

PUBLISHING + DESIGN

Get Up, Get Going: Tales of a Country Veterinarian. Copyright © 2019 by Dr. A.J. Neumann, D.V.M., and Renae B. Vander Schaaf. All rights reserved. No part of this book may be used or reproduced in any manner whatsoever without written permission from the author, except in the case of brief quotations embodied in critical articles or reviews.

Print ISBN: 978-1-7323526-3-6
E-Book ISBN: 978-1-7323526-6-7

Library of Congress Control Number: 2018914748

Published in the United States of America by the Write Place, Inc. For more information, please contact:

the Write Place, Inc.
809 W. 8th Street, Suite 2
Pella, Iowa 50219
www.thewriteplace.biz

Cover and interior design by Michelle Stam and Alexis Thomas, the Write Place, Inc. Barn cover photo courtesy of Dan, Theresa, and Ryan Mc Carty.

Copies of this book may be ordered online at Amazon and BarnesandNoble.com.

View other Write Place titles at www.thewriteplace.biz.

DEDICATION

I took this picture of my parents, Frederick and Nettie Neumann, one day when I was home from college in 1948. They had just been out working in the garden. It is truly a portrait of them as they were.

My parents worked hard their entire lives. Family was very important to them, and it took a great deal of self-sacrificing to raise their nine children. They read the Bible and lived their lives accordingly, teaching us through their example. From them, we learned the value of thriftiness, working hard, and always meeting our obligations.

CONTENTS

Prologue i

PART I — THE EARLY YEARS

Chapter One: The Year Was 1926 11
Chapter Two: Chores 19
Chapter Three: Family 27
Chapter Four: Making Do During the Depression 37
Chapter Five: Neighbors..49
Chapter Six: Adventurous, Mischievous, or Just Plain Naughty 55
Chapter Seven: High School..69
Chapter Eight: Off to College 77
Chapter Nine: Off to the Military 83

PART II — THE CLINIC YEARS

Chapter Ten: You Are Moving Where? Never Heard of That Town. 93
Chapter Eleven: Who Is That Girl? 99
Chapter Twelve: A Home of Our Own..109
Chapter Thirteen: Mary, My Partner..115
Chapter Fourteen: Early Calls... 127
Chapter Fifteen: Some Extra-Memorable Calls, Part I 133
Chapter Sixteen: Some Extra-Memorable Calls, Part II 141
Chapter Seventeen: A Few Trips to the Emergency Room 153
Chapter Eighteen: Sometimes an Animal Can Be Dangerous 161
Chapter Nineteen: A Veterinary Clinic Grows.............................181
Chapter Twenty: Just What Is Going On? 193

PART III — THE DRAFT HORSE YEARS

Chapter Twenty-One: Belgian Draft Horses 201

Chapter Twenty-Two: Memories of a Horse Doc 213

Chapter Twenty-Three: Horse Observations 221

Chapter Twenty-Four: *Draft Horse Journal*, Horse Clinics,
    and Judging Fairs...229

Chapter Twenty-Five: "Mary, We Are Going to Australia!" 249

Chapter Twenty-Six: An Invitation to Colombia 259

Chapter Twenty-Seven: His Mules, His Horses, His Antiques................ 271

Chapter Twenty-Eight: My Rock of Gibraltar 283

Epilogue 285

PROLOGUE

Why Is This Man Still Alive?

(March 1958)

The only sound in the surgical room was the ticking of the clock. There was no reason for me, the man lying there, to be alive. But I was…barely.

The doctor gave my wife no assurance that I would *still* be alive in the morning. Instead, he urged her to go home. He said she needed her rest for the days ahead—plus, our children needed her. A family friend, Dr. Osdoba, promised to stay at the hospital and call her if there was any change.

It had been a dandy March day, the kind Northwest Iowa cherishes. The winter snow was gone, and the air was fresh and clear—just the kind of day where girls skip home from school and boys can't wait to change into chore clothes and explore the outdoors.

Farmers were happy to be back on the tractor, getting an early start on field work. It was just one gorgeous day.

I was busy going from one appointment to another. In the afternoon, I stopped at home to have dinner with my wife, Mary. We argued. She wanted me to take our son, David, along with me after we ate. She had something planned that a two-and-a-half-year-old boy would *not* appreciate going to. After all, David was a pistol—a rambunctious little boy.

"I don't see why you can't take him," said Mary Virginia.

"No, today just doesn't work," I replied.

"Neumann," said Mary (that was her name for me). "You are being unreasonable."

"Mary Virginia, normally I would be happy to take him," I answered. "He is a good boy, and I enjoy my time with him; but today, I just don't want him along."

"So you have no good reason for not taking him," said Mary, clearly annoyed. "And yet you won't? I don't understand you."

The more she persisted, the more adamant my "no" became.

"I am not taking David with me," I retorted. "And that's that."

With those words, I stormed out of the house. I slammed the door extra hard, leaving without eating my dinner.

Back in the car I used for my veterinary practice, I stopped at the office to restock supplies and check the call list.

While heading to my next call, I came upon an elderly couple stopped alongside the gravel road with a flat tire. I pulled over to help.

"Oh, you don't need to help us," they said.

"Someday I am going to meet my Maker," I replied carelessly. "I think this might help my case."

Once the tire was back on, I started down the road again, whistling a cheery tune.

Shortly after 3:30 p.m., another elderly couple left Orange City. They had been to the dentist. After finishing their shopping and errands in town, they headed north on K64 to their home in Sioux Center. A patrolman followed them through town, observing that they had not completely stopped at the stop signs. But he did not stop them.

When the couple left Orange City, a farmer driving a pickup started following their car north on the blacktop road. I was coming from the north, heading south on the blacktop.

As I entered the intersection where K64 and B40 meet, the farmer saw the elderly couple's car pull into the southbound lane to make a left turn.

But the southbound lane was not a turning lane.

I attempted to avoid a head-on collision by jamming on the brakes and turning toward the ditch, but there wasn't enough time or space.

My station wagon collided with their car, forcing it backwards on the road, while my crumpled-up vehicle landed in the ditch. The vet supplies in the back of the car went flying forward. The engine was pushed into the front passenger seat...

Right where David would have been sitting had he ridden along that afternoon.

Immediately, the farmer who had been following the elderly couple's car stopped to help. He was soon joined by Jake Vande Griend, whose farm was just north of the corner, and a Watkin's dealer who had been travelling on the road, visiting his clients.

From the appearance of the two smashed cars, the men did not think anyone could have survived the accident. The elderly couple did not.

Upon their first surveillance of the crash, they did not know where the driver of the second car (me) had ended up. They looked around, expecting to find me lying on the grass. But when they heard a sound coming from the car, they rushed over. I had been so covered with vet supplies—drugs and equipment—that they hadn't been able to see me. They pulled my unconscious body from the car and laid me on the grassy shoulder of the road. They were afraid my car might start to burn.

I was transported to the Grossman Bushmer Hospital in Orange City by the ambulance, which at the time was the hearse owned by the Van Etten Funeral Home. Dr. E.B. Grossman immediately came to the emergency room to examine me.

After the examination and initial care, I was placed in a room with another patient. I was still unconscious, but I was restless and groaning. The other patient complained, so I was moved to the surgical room. Because the hospital was full, there was no other place to put me. I remained there in the surgical room, unconscious, all night.

A nurse checked on me from time to time. Sometimes, she thought I was conscious and would ask if I could count to ten. I never responded to her.

It was around 8:00 a.m. the next morning when I woke up. I was lying on my back, and the first thing I saw was the ceiling lights. I had no clue where I was or how I had gotten there.

"Where am I?" I asked.

"Can you count to ten?" replied the nurse.

"One, two, three, four, five, six, seven, eight, nine, ten."

The nurse was so excited she ran out of the room to find a doctor.

Dr. Grossman came in and examined me. When he realized I had no recollection of the previous three days, he only told me I had been in a car accident. My status was critical, so he hesitated to tell me what had happened to the occupants of the other car when I asked about them.

They moved me to a regular room. My wife visited, but she had been told not to say anything about the accident.

Later that day, Dr. Grossman, Dr. Bushmer, and a nurse came in and told me what they knew of the details of the accident, including that the other couple had died.

Dr. Grossman then described my numerous injuries:

- All ribs on left side broken
- Right wrist shattered
- Front upper teeth knocked out
- Left kneecap broken
- Right eyeball knocked out
- Smashed face
- Concussion, possible serious head injury

If I survived, I would have a long, painful recovery. The doctor promised me they would do their best to minimize the pain. But he gave no promises as to my eyesight, as they had merely popped the eyeball back in. For now, my eyelid was sewn shut.

The medical staff refused to let me have a mirror to see my face. They said I would need plastic surgery.

"Who was with me last night?" I asked when they were finished delivering their prognosis.

"Dr. Osdoba stayed for a while," they answered.

"No, there was someone else," I said. "I didn't recognize his voice."

"There was no one else," they assured me. "If you heard something, it was just the workings of your mind."

"I *distinctly* remember hearing a man's voice," I firmly replied. "He said, 'Don't worry. You will be all right.' Then he recited Psalm 23 to me."

The doctors couldn't explain it, nor could they explain why my face, kneecap, and ribs healed so quickly. They were especially mystified as to why I didn't need any pain medication. The most surprising part of all?

All this healing occurred within a week.

They took the stitches out of my eyelid four or five days after the wreck. I could count the bricks on the building outside my window. My eyesight was almost normal. The only difference was that before the accident I didn't need glasses. Now I did.

The doctors couldn't believe it; they just grinned and said it was amazing.

The only problem I still had was my wrist. It would not bend properly. An appointment was made to see an orthopedic surgeon in Sioux Falls. I took my X-rays along.

After an examination, the orthopedic surgeon didn't offer much hope.

"The X-rays show that your wrist will always be stiff and impaired," he said.

"Is there anything you can do?" I asked. "I would like to have normal movement."

"No," he answered. "In time, the bones will fuse together naturally, but we can hasten that process with surgery."

That answer was unacceptable to me, so I left.

I remembered the voice I had heard that night in the hospital: "You will be all right." I knew my ribs, knee, and face had healed quickly and without pain. I was sure some proper movement in my wrist would be restored eventually.

Each evening, in the basement of my home, I began to work on that wrist. I would put my left hand on my right hand, working to bend it. In time, the wrist healed. Today, nearly sixty years later, the only difference is the injured wrist is a bit thicker than the other.

I felt blessed. I was working again, and my son was still alive. He never would have survived the accident if he had been along.

In the succeeding years, I would ponder many times the voice I heard that night: "Don't worry. You will be all right."

Psalm 23
A Psalm of David

The LORD is my shepherd; I shall not want.

He maketh me to lie down in green pastures: he leadeth me beside the still waters.

He restoreth my soul: he leadeth me in the paths of righteousness for his name's sake.

Yea, though I walk through the valley of the shadow of death, I will fear no evil: for thou art with me; thy rod and thy staff they comfort me.

Thou preparest a table before me in the presence of mine enemies: thou anointest my head with oil; my cup runneth over.

Surely goodness and mercy shall follow me all the days of my life: and I will dwell in the house of the LORD forever.

PART I

The Early Years

CHAPTER ONE

The Year Was 1926

The year was 1926. In February, President Calvin Coolidge had signed the Revenue Act, reducing income and inheritance taxes. On July 4, the United States celebrated its 150th birthday. Workers at the Ford factories went to a forty-hour, five-day week and earned six dollars a day. There was much to celebrate.

But for Frederick Carl Neumann and his wife, Nettie Adel (Maybohm) Neumann, their biggest joy came on June 24 when their first son, Arlo John, was born. I was their second child. My sister, Marjorie, was four years old at the time. Dr. Armstrong and midwife/nurse Mae Tompkins were there to assist my mother with my arrival.

I received my first complimentary slap on my bottom in this room. It was the first of many to come. (My parents administered discipline by the brass bed in the downstairs bedroom. I received my fair share.)

PRESTON, IOWA

Our home was on the edge of a little Iowa town called Preston, located in Jackson County. The town is twelve miles west of the Mississippi River and thirty-three miles south of Dubuque. The Maquoketa River runs its course to the Mississippi River northeast of town.

In 1926, Preston was thriving. We had anything anyone ever needed: two blacksmith shops, a car dealership, a doctor, a dentist, a veterinarian, a lawyer, clothing stores, shoe stores, grocery stores, a school, and a grain elevator. There were four churches: Catholic, Congregationalist, Lutheran, and Methodist. A train depot connected Preston with the world. It was on the Milwaukee rail line. (We called it the Milwaukee Road.) Each day, two passenger trains and one freight train stopped in town.

There wasn't much reason to go anywhere else.

MY SIBLINGS

Fourteen months after I was born, my brother, Darryl, made his appearance. We were comrades in work and play. If one was in trouble, the other brother was probably involved.

Eventually the Neumann family would grow to include Cleo, Shirley, Nancy, Frederick, Karen, and Carl. Carl was born in a hospital in 1943. Times were indeed changing.

Karen's birth gave me a little bit of trouble. (Yes, me—not my mother).

It was a miserable, messy Leap Year Day—no sunshine, but still plenty of thawing. The moisture in the air made everything dismal and sloppy.

When I got to the door of our house after walking home from school, my mother did not meet me. Instead I saw Mae Tompkins, the neighbor lady.

"Your mother has something to show you," she said. She directed me to the bedroom.

"Look at what we have here!" said my happy mother, holding Karen out for me to see.

"Oh *no*, not another one!" I blurted.

That didn't go over too well. Darryl and I often had to watch the younger ones—especially when we thought we had better things to

Me riding my broom horse and sticking up my brother Darryl, who has candy. Our neighbor, Dr. Roach, saw us playing and had us pose for this picture.

do—which explains my dismay. Since then I have learned to not be quite so blunt in sharing my first thoughts. I love Karen, dearly. We talk on the telephone and visit as much as we are able. She has lived in Preston her whole life.

MY HOME

Our first home was an old two-story house. Like many homes of the day, it did not have running water or indoor plumbing. We used an outhouse. That little building was mighty important, and life was rather inconvenient when one had to be without it. (We'll get to that story later.)

The kitchen had a wood or cob stove that heated the room very well. That was good in the winter, but in the summer it did get a bit hot. Mother used the cob stove for cooking and canning until I was about ten or twelve years old. Then she got a gas stove, though for some time she used both.

We ate our meals and took our baths in the kitchen. Saturday night was bath night, whether we needed one or not. We carried water in from the faucet outside. We'd then fill a copper boiler with water and heat it on top of the stove. That water was supplemented with hot water from the stove's reservoir. The girls took their bath first, the boys last.

We never had indoor plumbing while we lived in that house. But we did have running water—someone had to run after it.

We only used the living room when there were visitors. Otherwise it was off-limits to everyone. It also went unheated unless we had guests. In that case, a parlor stove warmed the living room and a small room that also served as the guest bedroom. The stove burned wood or coal, but we mostly used wood since coal cost money.

The dining room was also heated with a wood- or coal-burning stove. The same stove heated my parents' bedroom. The stovepipe ran upstairs through the girls' bedroom, thereby providing them with heat as well.

The girls' room was the biggest, and one of four rooms upstairs. Darryl and I also had a room upstairs, but sometimes we moved our double bed to the head of the stairs to get heat or a breeze. It was very cold in the winter and hot in the summer.

In the fall, Mother would put flannel sheets on all the beds. To stay warm, we also slept in flannel pajamas under a feather tick, which was a poor man's down blanket. Mother made the feather ticks using down from ducks and geese. She would stuff it into durable, blue-and-white-striped mattress material.

Every morning, Dad would open the door to the stairs and give us his wake-up call:

"Boys."

We usually didn't dally long, but if for some reason he had to call a second time, he would do so more forcefully…and we would hit the ground running.

When the weather was cold, we would quickly grab our clothes and hurry down to the warm stove in the dining room. We dressed in the space between the stove and the wall.

THE CELLAR

The cellar had a cement floor and stone walls. There was an outdoor entrance, which was very nice when we were bringing in bushels of potatoes and apples. In the dining room, there were also steps going to the cellar.

We stored canned jars of fruits, meats, and vegetables in the cellar. We dried apples from our Greening and Jonathon trees with sulfur. There were a couple of big wooden bins that we filled with potatoes from the garden.

One time, Dad and a neighbor decided to make some home brew. They made it, bottled it, and put it on the shelves in our cellar. Sometime later, my folks asked our other neighbors, Dr. and Mrs. Roach, over to play cards. The Roaches didn't believe in drinking alcoholic beverages at any time.

The two couples were sitting at the dining room table, playing cards. Darryl and I were hanging around when we heard a funny explosion in the cellar, one *boom* followed by another.

"Boys, go see what is happening in the cellar," called Dad.

We immediately obeyed and found the home brew fermenting, blowing the corks off the bottles. There was a sticky mess all over.

We had a problem. Darryl and I knew our neighbors were adamantly opposed to alcohol, so we didn't dare tell Dad his homemade brew was exploding in front of the company. We got his attention and motioned for him to come over, so we could tell him without the Roaches knowing.

Dad fabricated some excuse to leave the room and check things out in the basement. Once he realized what was happening, he came up with a story to hustle the Roaches out. We cleaned up the mess and saved what we could.

My mother canned and *canned* everything. It was a big job to put up enough food for the winter, in addition to what we would eat the rest of the year. We could grow our own apples but had to purchase lugs of peaches and pears. We made our own sauerkraut from the cabbage in the garden. It was stored in crocks in the cellar.

Mother took great pride in having the cellar full of food for the winter. I remember one time she took us all down there and said, "Look, I have canned a thousand jars of produce."

And remember, she did it all on the cook stove and without air conditioning. It was real work.

THE GARDEN

Everyone helped in the garden. It took a lot of hoeing, digging potatoes, and picking beans and peas to keep us fed. We even grew our own popcorn. A favorite for many years was Japanese Hulless. We also grew a strawberry popcorn variety, which was a short and stubby red ear.

Dad would work all day at his masonry job. Then after supper he would say, "Boys, let's go out and do some hoeing and weeding in the garden." We did, but it took away any free time we may have had in the evening.

BUTCHERING

Besides having a cellar and a big garden, we also did our own butchering. We would do one beef cow and four or five hogs in February. Sometimes Dad also butchered for other families. Darryl and I would often go along to assist.

Butchering days were extra busy. We would fill the smokehouse with pork shoulders, bacon, and hams. In the summer, when the weather turned warm, the smoked meat would start to drip and needed to be used up. We didn't have an ice box, so there were days when we would have smoked meat for all three meals.

Friends and relatives would come to help "cold pack" the meat, which meant cooking the meat before layering it in a crock. Each layer would be covered with freshly rendered lard before the next layer of meat was placed on top. So it went—meat, lard, meat, lard—until the crock was filled. The final layer was lard, which sealed it all in. The crocks sat in the coldest spot in the cellar. A good portion of the beef was canned. A smaller amount of beef was preserved in a crock. Most of the pork was either smoked or cold packed.

As long as it remained cold during the winter, some meat could be stored outside in a box on the north side of the house. If snow was on the ground, we would shovel it over this box to help insulate the meat.

Even the blood was saved during butchering and made into blood sausage. In 2008, my wife and I made a trip to Germany, to my ancestral home. When they asked me what I wanted for breakfast, I asked if it would be possible to have blood sausage.

"Yes," my host answered. "We can do that. There is a local meat market that has been in business for over six hundred years and still makes blood sausage."

It was very good, and I made it my breakfast meat for several days.

Certain parts from the hogs went into another delicacy, one with the descriptive title of head cheese.* The trimmings were ground and mixed together with salt and pepper. Then the whole thing was placed in a pan and later sliced and fried. It was quite tasty! Beef and pork brains were also sliced and rolled in bread crumbs or flour before frying. Nothing was wasted.

My parents raised a lot of chickens for meat and eggs, usually growing the larger breeds like Black Jersey Giants and Rhode Island Reds. The baby chicks were bought at a local store. Some years we raised ducks and geese, but never turkeys. A turkey was purchased once a year at Thanksgiving.

One unique thing my mother did was pickle chicken. It was eaten cold. Mother would take it right from the jar and put it in a bowl to serve. You could choose a drumstick, wing, or whatever part of the chicken you desired. I have never seen pickled chicken anywhere else. When I mention it, most people have never heard of it. Once I left home, I never ate pickled chicken again.

Many Saturday nights, especially in the winter, Darryl and I were sent to the chicken house, where the chickens were roosting. By lantern light, we would choose two big roosters to butcher for the Sunday meal. Mother always roasted them in the cook stove's oven.

One year, a bobwhite quail found its way into our chicken house. Each night, just before it was time to shut the door, the quail would come in and hide itself between a rooster or a hen's legs. When we were selecting a fowl for the next day's meal, we always left the one sheltering the quail and moved on to a different bird.

Or "grits," as it was called in my family. But the word "grits" is more often associated with the Southern dish of hot cereal made from hominy or corn.

CHAPTER TWO

Chores

Like most boys growing up in the thirties, there was always plenty of work to do. And not only for me, but for everyone. Almost every family fought to keep the wolf from the door.

DAILY TASKS

The cows were milked twice a day. We sold milk to others in town who didn't keep a cow. We separated the cream from the milk with a cream separator, making skim milk that was fed to the hogs to fatten them up. The cream was then either sold to the Preston Creamery or used to make butter.

Some days, when Darryl and I got home from school, Mother would say to us, "Boys, before you change into your chore clothes, I want you to churn some butter." She would have it all ready to go; we took turns turning the handle on the Dazey glass butter churn.

We also regularly cleaned out the cattle and hog barns with a manure fork and scoop shovel. Cleaning the chicken coop was the worst job because of the strong ammonia smell.

If there wasn't garden work, our father might suggest we mow the lawn. At first, the mowing was done with an old Eclipse mower.

Later we got a real fancy model, another Eclipse with rubber tires. I wasn't sure it pushed any easier than the steel-wheeled model, though.

CULTIVATING

Every morning during cultivating season, our father would say before he went off to work, "Boys, I want this many rows of corn cultivated."

We knew he meant it.

After morning chores were done, we would hook up our one-row cultivator to the old horse team, a white and a bay. Father had changed the handles on the Jenny Lind cultivator so we each could hold a handle as the shovel took out weeds between the corn rows.

The old team of horses knew more about cultivating than we did. When they came to the end of the row, they would stop. After we got the shovels up, with a little urging they would swing around into the next row pretty much by themselves. They would stop again and wait for the command to go. The good ol' team didn't need any guidance, so they were just what we two young boys needed. We often did an extra row or two for good measure.

I am pretty sure farmers had a good laugh when they saw our way of cultivating.

SOYBEANS

One year, my dad tried a new crop called "soybeans." It was the first time I ever saw soybeans. They weren't planted in rows, like they are today. Instead, farmers broadcasted the seed and mowed it while it was still green, so the beans would stay in the pods. After they dried, we put the soybeans up as loose hay to be stored in the barn. It proved to be too rich to use alone as feed, so it was mixed with straw or poor-quality hay.

THE TIMBER

Winter in eastern Iowa can be cold, so Dad made sure we had plenty of cut wood to keep the stoves going.

We usually went to the timber in the fall to get wood. The timber belonged to farmers who wanted certain trees thinned so their cattle had more room to graze. Most of the time, the timber was three to four miles from our home; but at times we would go out as far as fifteen miles. One time, we cut a whole stand of shagbark hickory for firewood because someone wanted it cut. It would have made good lumber, as the trunks stood approximately 30 feet before the first branch.

Hickory was the best tree for firewood. Then oak, followed by elm. The trees we cut were fully matured, with trunks 2.5 feet in diameter.

Darryl and I would cut really big oak trees with a crosscut saw. After the trunk had been blasted open, we split the log with a maul (sledge hammer) and wedge. Sometimes the logs were split into eight-foot lengths for making fence posts. We would set the posts on end so the air could circulate around them to dry the wood. Any remaining bark was chopped off with a hatchet, because the posts would rot more quickly if the bark was left on.

Dad did a lot of the trimming that required an axe, while Darryl and I trimmed the larger branches off with the crosscut saw. The wood was cut into ten- or twelve-foot lengths and placed on a pile. When the wood had dried some, it was brought home. After chores and supper, Dad would say, "Boys, let's go run some wood through the buzz saw."

The buzz saw was engine-powered and would cut the wood into blocks for stoves or furnaces. We sold some of the wood to homes and businesses. Darryl and I stacked it in the basements or store rooms of our customers. We delivered the wood with a horse and wagon until Dad saved $400. With that money, he bought a brand-new red 1936 International pickup. Then we delivered the wood in style.

The International pickup was our only motor vehicle for several years.

WHISKEY BARRELS

One time, some men came through our neighborhood to buy white oak trees of a certain size. Prohibition had ended on December 5, 1933; there were whiskey manufacturers who wanted the lumber for their barrels. They only wanted the butt, or trunk, of the tree, not the branch wood.

Marked white oaks were scattered throughout the woods. After they were cut down, the trees were all cut into eight- or ten-foot sections. The farmers were paid another ten cents per log when they delivered the lumber to the loading zones. Most of the farmers used a team of horses to drag one log at a time. The logs were later picked up by a truck.

Darryl and I were quite young, maybe ten and eleven years old, when we started our first log-skidding operation to help with this project. Friends of the family offered the job to us. They probably could have done it themselves, but they chose to let us do the work to help the family during these financially tough times. Dad gave us his permission. We hooked up the team and went to work. We had to chain up each log before pulling it out of the woods and hauling it to a loading zone. Dad gave us strict orders that the horses were *not* to get hurt.

This project was definitely something different to do, and we were paid for the work we did.

HUNTING

I really enjoyed walking in the timber. It was there that Darryl and I did the majority of our hunting. We hunted pheasants, quail, rabbits, and squirrels. We didn't hunt deer, for in those days it was rare to see a deer. We didn't hunt for sport; all the game we shot, we ate.

It took five or six squirrels to feed our family. Mother browned them in the frying pan with butter or lard before putting them in a roaster in the oven. She cooked them until the meat was ready to come off the bone. She did the same with rabbit, quail, and pheasant.

Squirrel hunting was done mainly in the timber, which was home to small gray squirrels and large red fox squirrels. The little gray squirrels were a lot faster and more difficult to shoot. One of us carried the shotgun and the other the .22. We would walk parallel to each other, some distance apart. We had it down pat. When the squirrel would go around the tree to hide from one of us, the other one could see it. And then we usually had squirrel to eat.

We would go to the fields and pick up fox tracks after a fresh snow, if we had time or school was cancelled. We would trail him until we either procured him or he got away. They could outfox us. Coyotes were rarely seen in eastern Iowa at that time.

A TRAP LINE

In addition to hunting, Darryl and I "ran" a trap line, which was our best enterprise. We trapped beavers, minks, muskrats, raccoons, and skunks. At the end of the season, we sold the furs to a buyer in Maquoketa. One winter we earned over $400. (Fur prices were high because the war was going on.)

Trapping was just one of the many things Dad taught us. Even though he helped us, we were allowed to keep any money we earned from our trap line. (At that time, many boys had to turn the money they made over to their parents.)

The trapping season began in early October or November. Copper Creek ran through our land; Dad had talked to the farmers up and down the creek, and we had permission to run trap lines for three miles.

After morning chores were done, but before breakfast, we ran the trap lines. I usually took the northern one-and-a-half miles while Darryl did the other trap line. We did most of the skinning ourselves, with occasional help from Dad. One subzero winter morning, when the creek was covered with ice, I fell through into waist-deep water. Needless to say, I ran home, freezing all the way.

But, we were *never* late for school.

FISHING

If we had time, we went fishing, sometimes in Copper Creek and sometimes in the Mississippi River, which was twelve miles east. Another favorite place was Green Island. It was a special treat to go to this huge natural slough where the Maquoketa River entered the Mississippi River.

Green Island was a great spot for hunting ducks and fishing. Rough fish, crappies, bass, bull heads, and catfish were the main catches we brought home for supper. I once hooked a forty-nine-pound catfish. When we were younger, we fished from the shore; but when we got older Dad outfitted us with a small boat. Like hunting, fishing was not just recreation. It was food for the family.

CLEANING HORSE STALLS

Sometimes we worked for other farmers, though Dad was a bit choosy about who we worked for. One of our favorite neighbors was Johannes Moellenhof. He was an old-timer, a tough man in an honest way. He spoke a mixture of English and German and had the habit of saying, "By Jinkels, boys. That beats the Hell." When we had a free Saturday afternoon, he paid us fifty cents to clean his horse stalls .

Mr. Moellenhof, as we called him, was a dairy farmer who delivered milk every morning with his white Percheron horse and wagon. The horse knew the route. They would enter a block and Johannes would fill quart jars with milk from the cans in his wagon. The heavy wire milk carrier held a half-dozen quarts of milk. He would carry this from house to house, leaving as many quarts as the household had ordered. The horse would walk ahead on his own to where he knew Johannes would need to restock his bottled milk supply.

PAPER ROUTE

One summer, Darryl and I delivered the *Des Moines Register* Sunday newspaper. We would hurry down to the train station early Sunday morning to meet the train that carried the paper.

The train went through our town *lickety-split*. It did not stop; the workers in the mail car simply opened the door when they got near the depot to throw out bundles of newspapers tied in twine and wrapped in some covering. We had to be quick to have the newspapers delivered along our route before church.

CLEANING THE BARBERSHOP

We also cleaned the barbershop on Sunday afternoons. When I was young, Saturday evening was the biggest time for barbers. Farmers would come to town, and the barbers would sometimes cut hair until after midnight. We would sweep the floors and do other general cleaning. As I remember, it was hard work.

HAYING

During haying season, it was not uncommon for farmers to stop at our home to see if the boys could help with the hay harvest.

We boys would drive horses to rake hay or pull the hay rack. But mostly the farmers we worked for put us in the haymow. It was hard, sweaty work.

The hay was brought to the barn on a hay wagon pulled by a team of horses. The loose hay was then pulled up with a hay fork or a big sling. Both were popular. As the hay went down the track in the barn, we would yell when it was time to pull the rope to empty the hay fork or sling. The hay would be dumped in a pile in the middle of the mow. We would then fork the hay to the sides. It seemed like whenever we had the load done, we would look out the haymow door to see another load coming in.

We worked stripped down to the waist, as we would sweat profusely. Usually, there was a cream can full of water in the mow. We would take the dipper out and pour water over our heads to cool off.

One time, when we were mowing hay for the Rubel family, I happened to look out the other side of the barn. I saw Mrs. Harry Rubel cultivating with a single-row riding cultivator. She had a young child sitting on her lap. One horse was not pulling his share. Mrs. Rubel had to keep encouraging him by tapping him on the rump with a bamboo fishing pole. She had her hands full.

But that's how the work got done. Men, women, and children all did their share.

CHAPTER THREE

Family

I had a good childhood, thanks to my family. We worked hard, but we also enjoyed just spending time together.

For example, there were frequent gatherings with grandma, uncles, aunts, and cousins. Some were impromptu, while others were more routine. After church on Sunday, we often gathered at a city park or someone's home. Everyone contributed a tasty dish of food to eat. Mom often roasted chicken. Pies were the standard dessert. Weather permitting, my dad, uncles, and cousins would relax with a friendly game of softball in our pasture.

MY MOTHER'S ANCESTRY

My mother, Nettie Adel (Maybohm) Neumann, was raised approximately fifteen miles from Preston—in a little town in Clinton County called Bryant. Her dad, John W. Maybohm, came to America alone at age fifteen. He was originally from an area in Germany near the Belgian border. That is all the background information we have on him. My parents gave me the middle name of John in his honor.

John Maybohm worked as a mechanic for a business that repaired farm machinery in Ten Mile House, a town two miles from Bryant. Ten Mile House received its name because it was where stage coaches stopped for fresh horses on the road between Clinton and Maquoketa.

Later, when cars became popular, John worked on them instead of farm equipment. His two sons owned and operated the Ford dealership in Preston. John Maybohm died after WWI from an abscess on his lungs. I never knew him.

I do remember Grandma Annie Maybohm. She was a Thielen before her marriage, born in eastern Iowa. She ran a restaurant in Bryant. Later, when the family moved to Preston, they ran a restaurant in that town.

I also remember Grandma Maybohm's mother—my great-grandmother, who was a determined woman. They lived together in an apartment above the Preston post office after Grandpa Maybohm passed away.

In the spring, we all had to take a tonic—Grandma's orders. Feisty little Grandma Maybohm would call when it was time for the tonic to be administered, and we all had to be at home when she arrived. We would soon see her coming down the street with her big black pocketbook in one hand and a bag with her spring tonic in the other.

We stood in line to get Grandma's spring tonic. It tasted awful! It had the cleansing power of a laxative, and the ingredients were her secret. There might have been some benefits to it though, as Grandma lived into her nineties. She and Grandpa Maybohm are buried in Ingwersen Cemetery, near Ten Mile House.

MY FATHER'S ANCESTRY

My dad was the youngest of four children. His mother, Julie Pilscheur Neumann, died when he was seven years old. She had come to America in 1892 with her husband, Friedrich Neumann—my father's namesake.

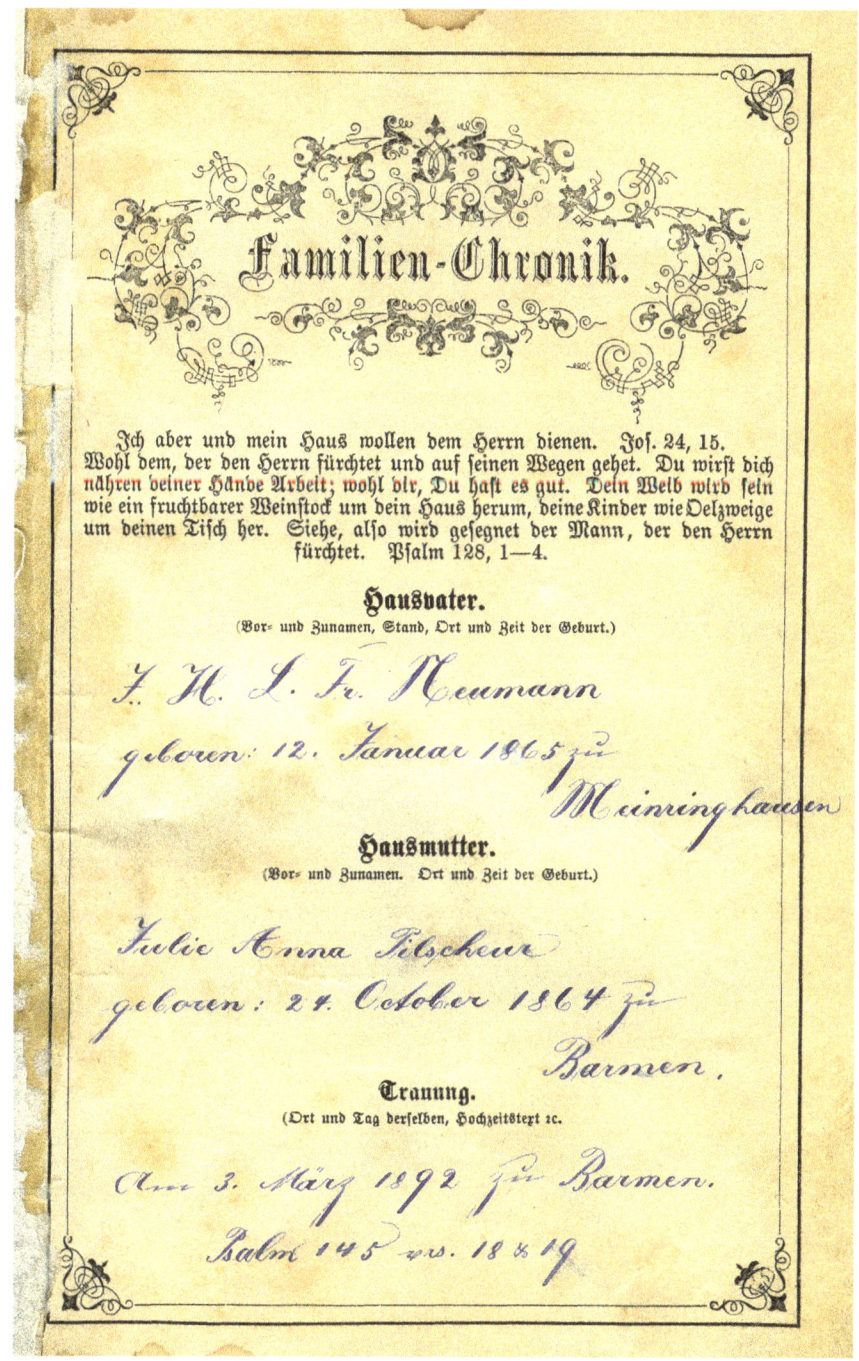

A page from the Bible brought to America by my grandfather and grandmother, Friedrich Carl and Julie Neumann.

Julie Anna Pilscheur Neumann was born to Gustaf and Wilhelmine Pilscheur on October 24, 1864, in Barmen, Germany. Gustaf was a *Färber*—a dyer. He owned a textile-dying business. Julie married Friedrich in the Lutheran church in Barmen on March 3, 1892. Barmen is an industrial town situated in the Wupper River Valley, now referred to as Wuppertal. Wuppertal was fire-bombed in World War II. Several of my relatives were maimed or killed during these attacks.

My grandfather's full name was Johannes Heinrich Ludwig Friedrich Neumann. He was born to Johannes and Friederike Neumann on January 12, 1865, in a village named Meineringhausen. At that time, Meineringhausen was located in Prussia, but it is now part of Germany. It is a small village in the province of Waldeck. Meineringhausen dates back to the Viking era. It is situated on the crest of a small hill, where the tree of Thor once stood. The Church of Meineringhausen now stands in the tree's place and is surrounded by houses. (Meineringhausen literally means "my ring of houses.") If someone asked my grandfather where he came from, he probably would have replied, *"Ich bein Waldecker…I am a Waldecker."*

Friedrich's father, Johannes, was a farmer. Grandpa Friedrich was one of their five surviving children. His sister, Auguste, stayed on the family farm. His brother, Heinrich, and sister, Louise, moved to Barmen. Youngest brother Carl immigrated to the United States with Friedrich and Julie in 1892. Carl was then only twelve years old.

I have a relative who still lives in the house where my grandfather was born. He is a fourth-generation shepherd. We visited him in 2008. During the day, he would take the sheep out to pasture. He and two dogs would keep watch over the flock. At night, the sheep were brought back to the barn.

The house and barn were both in the village, which was quite common in the area. We saw very few buildings in the countryside, or even fences. Seldom are any buildings built on farmland in that part of Germany.

The countryside around Meineringhausen looks very similar to eastern Iowa, with open fields and forests. We could see how our grandparents felt at home near Preston.

MOM AND DAD'S WORK

Mom was a good cook. We ate well throughout the Depression years because we raised our own food—meat, milk, eggs, fruits, and vegetables. Mom was always busy baking cakes, rolls, and pies.

Oh, it was a happy day when she baked bread! We ate it with honey and butter while it was still warm. Then, when one of us had a birthday, Mom made us our special pie. My dad's pie was lemon meringue; mine was mincemeat.

Mother also sewed all our clothes. All us boys wore overalls to school. Once home, we took our clean pair of overalls off and changed into chore clothes. We went barefoot as much as possible, so our feet were tough. We could run over rocks and all kinds of things. Our neighbor—Dr. Roach, a veterinarian—once said to Mom, "Nettie, those children do not need shoes. Let them go barefoot. They won't have foot problems when they grow up."

Like his father, Dad was a mason—a brick layer. My grandfather had learned the skill during his youth in Germany. When he immigrated to the United States, he continued the vocation, teaching it to his son. My dad carried on the tradition, teaching masonry to all four of his sons. My brother, Darryl, remained a mason all his life. He worked on my house in Orange City, including the plaster, which is still flawless after fifty years.

One of our father and grandfather's proudest achievements was building St. John's Evangelical Lutheran Church in Preston. This is where our family attended church each Sunday and where I was confirmed one Easter Sunday.

MAKING HOLIDAY CELEBRATIONS SPECIAL

Thanksgiving and Christmas were celebrations for the whole family. My mother always made oyster stew for supper on Christmas Eve. After supper, we walked to the Lutheran church for the Christmas program. (There was always a Neumann child in the program.) A tall evergreen from a local farmer would be on display, reaching the ceiling and filling the whole church with its fragrance and grandeur. To get it in the door, the tree's limbs had to be rolled tight. There were always presents underneath it.

After church, a large group—the Roaches, the Tompkins, my mother's sister and her family from Clinton, two married uncles who had no children, and an aunt and uncle from Maquoketa with their four or five children—would all gather at the Neumann house. Our home would be filled with plenty of people and plenty of food.

The living room door would open to reveal a tree shining with candles and sheltering plenty of gifts. The candles were lit only once or twice during the holiday season, but the tree was fully decorated with many handmade ornaments. My parents always had plenty of buckets filled with water on hand, just in case a fire broke out. Years later, electric lights replaced the candles.

Christmas Day was celebrated at Grandma Maybohm's house. Many relatives gathered for the fellowship and big meal, which included roast duck, roast turkey, and roast goose. Grandma did a lot of the fixings, but she had some help from her children. As I remember, there were all kinds of pie!

One Christmas especially stands out. That year, my sister, Cleo, said there was no such person as Santa Claus. She was insistent that he didn't exist. In the days leading up to Christmas, the rest of the kids kept arguing with her that there *had* to be a Santa Claus.

Well, Christmas Eve proceeded as normal—oyster stew, church, and family visiting. Then the living room door opened, and suddenly a hush came over us. There were no gifts! Obviously, Santa hadn't been to our house yet. It was a very disappointing moment for us children. We were shocked and looked at each other in silence.

All of a sudden, we heard sleigh bells, followed by a loud thumping coming down the stairs that opened into the living room. It was, of course, Santa himself!

He had a white bag filled with gifts, which he handed out one by one with much laughter and merriment. When he gave Cleo hers, she choked out a surprised, "Thank you, Santa Claus!"

His bag empty, Santa said he had many more homes to visit. So, back up the stairs he went. Soon we heard the jingling sleigh bells again.

My parents suggested we children go up to have a look and see if we could catch a glimpse of his sleigh. We hurried to the window, but there was no trace of the kind old saint.

Cleo was once again a baptized believer.

My parents were poor, but they enjoyed doing things like this for their children. We later learned Santa had climbed a ladder up to an upstairs window and made his escape by climbing down again. He took the ladder with him, leaving no trace except a precious memory.

Santa was played by the local barber, Kenneth Roach, who was a bachelor at the time. He was rather heavyset—one could say he was built for the role. He played Santa Claus at various events in the area.

In short, I had a good childhood thanks to my family—lots of work and plenty of love.

The Neumann ancesteral barn and house in Germany.

My parents made sure we were in church every Sunday. I am the first boy in the front row, on the left.

The church I attended while growing up. My father and grandfather helped build it.
Photo courtesy of St. John's Evangelical Lutheran Church, Preston, Iowa.

CHAPTER FOUR

Making Do During the Depression

Lack of money was always a problem for our family during the Depression. Many of our neighbors were in the same boat. We all worked hard to maintain what we called a good life—food to eat and a roof over our heads.

MAKING DO: AN EXAMPLE

One time, when things were especially tight, my mother broke the glass chimney on the lamp. She could not afford to replace it, so she had us boys bring in a lantern from the barn. We cleaned it up and used that for our house light.

A few days later, our dad heard about a job scooping coal. He took his coal fork and joined the long line of men looking for a job to feed their families. Dad got the job and scooped coal all day.

When he came home that night, he was exhausted and hardly recognizable, covered from head to foot with coal dust.

But he laid a dime on the kitchen table by our mother. That was his pay for the day, and it was enough money to replace the lamp chimney.

A NEIGHBOR NEEDS HELP

Since I was born in 1926, much of my childhood was during the 1930s, also known as the Dust Bowl Years. Everyone worked to survive. No one had much money, so labor was often traded for goods or services. It was a time when neighbors needed neighbors and friends needed friends in order to meet life's challenges.

One afternoon, when we came home from school, Dad told Darryl and me to hurry through our chores. A neighbor needed his help, and he wanted us two boys to come along.

It had been an icy day; the neighbor's three-year-old draft colt had slipped, fracturing his front leg. The neighbor didn't know how to slaughter, nor could he afford to hire someone to do it for him. So he wanted Dad's help.

The colt was hopping along on three legs when we got there. We took the colt to the alleyway of the corncrib. Once the colt was put down, we used a block and tackle to lift him up. There my father and neighbor did the work of butchering and dressing out the meat.

For my dad's services, the neighbor gave us a hind quarter of meat. We took the meat home and hung it up in a shed to cool and age for about ten days. Later, we cut it up into roasts and steaks, just like we would have had it been a beef animal. Because it was winter, we were able to keep the meat fresh in an ice box outside.

Mother cooked it, but she wouldn't eat it. I thought the meat was very tasty. I could not tell the difference between beef and horse meat, except the horse meat was slightly darker and the fat was quite yellow in color.

SHARING WHAT WE HAD

My parents seldom went away on their own; they almost always took the family along. But there is one exception that stands out vividly in my mind.

The "Dirty Thirties" Dust Bowl did not affect eastern Iowa as much as it did western Iowa. My mother's sister, Bessie, and her husband, George, lived near Bronson, which is southeast of Sioux City. It was horribly dry there. The extreme drought and heat prevented my uncle and aunt from growing any crops. Even the garden dried up, despite their efforts to save it. They had been living off the ten-cent bounty their children earned from shooting starlings, paid by the clerk at the county courthouse.

That autumn, my parents filled up the little red International pickup with apples, potatoes, and all kinds of food—including some of my mother's home-canned goods.

I can remember them leaving us at home while they delivered this needed food to Uncle George, Aunt Bessie, and their children. They were gone for a couple days. It was the longest, farthest trip they made while I was growing up.

A FAVORITE DEPRESSION MEAL

At noon, when my siblings and I came home from school, we often ate this simple concoction.

We would prepare two soft-boiled eggs, a little butter, and some salt and pepper. This was all placed in a glass. Then we would add a few crushed saltine crackers. Bread crumbs would work too, but we always had crackers in our house. We would mix it all together with a fork and eat it from the glass.

That was our noon meal. It was really good; I still make it sometimes.

THE WPA

During the Depression years, many dams and locks were built on the Mississippi River as Works Progress Administration (WPA) projects. Like a lot of other men, my dad applied for one of these jobs. He worked the night shift on the dam at Bellevue.

This night-shift job of Dad's gave us many laughs. On his application, he wrote he was a cement worker. But he was given a job as an electrician...something he knew absolutely nothing about. We didn't even have electricity in our house! We just said, "That's the government for you."

With the WPA and the CCC, most of the work was done by hand. At one time, my dad was foreman of a WPA work crew assigned to a gravel quarry.

For many families, ours included, these jobs were a life-saver. All these jobs gave people the opportunity to work and earn at least some money. It helped them keep their dignity and self-respect, doing work that mattered. It wasn't just a handout.

DOCTORING DURING THE DEPRESSION

On the last Christmas we celebrated at Grandma Maybohm's house, the weather was so warm that we all played outdoors without wearing jackets or coats. There wasn't any snow.

Two days later, two of my sisters, Nancy and Shirley, came down with pneumonia. They were very sick. We seldom had the doctor out to our house, but this time my parents called either Dr. Armstrong or Dr. Dwyer. (They were the town's doctors.) Doctors made house calls in that day, and whoever my parents summoned came right over.

He instructed my parents to move the girls to the unused bedroom off the parlor. He then ordered them to open the windows and let plenty of the fresh, cold air into the unheated room. Our neighbor, Mae Tompkins, came over to help my mother with the nursing.

Antibiotics had not been developed yet, so the doctor asked them to treat my sisters with mustard-and-onion poultices. Onions were diced and mixed with mustard before lard or goose grease was added. This mixture was then either applied directly to the chest area or to a soft cloth like a diaper, which was wrapped around the chest so the lungs would benefit from the poultice.

Miss Tompkins also rubbed her goose grease and turpentine mixture under the girls' nostrils, just above their lips. My sisters were sick for two weeks, but they recovered completely.

Whenever we had a bad cold, we used the turpentine and goose grease if Vicks and Mentholatum were not available. These medications were rubbed into the neck, and a sock was wrapped around the area to hold the plaster in. It worked.

If we had a really bad cough, a half-ounce of whiskey was put in some water and heated. It tasted horrible, so we had to be forced to drink it. We nicknamed it a "hot toddy," but it was a standard treatment for a really bad cold.

We were not sick often. Sometimes I wonder if we benefited from sleeping in an ice-cold room under feather tick blankets.

DISEASES AND FUNERALS

Despite everyone's best efforts, it was nigh impossible to keep flies out of our homes. We sprayed, hung fly traps, used swatters—yet still they persisted. Sometimes we put lime down the toilet holes to cover up the breeding grounds there. It helped, but flies always seem to be present.

And they spread disease.

Everyone was plumb scared of polio. It was prevalent worldwide, and no one knew who would be struck next. Families were quarantined for polio, as well as chicken pox, measles, mumps, whooping cough, and scarlet fever. Paper was hung on the doors of quarantined families to let others know there was sickness in the house.

Tetanus was a problem, too. Whenever a Neumann child stepped on a nail, our parents made sure they got their tetanus shots. Other children's families didn't, and some children died.

If someone died, the undertaker would come and get the deceased. The Preston morticians were Mr. Campbell and Mr. Krabbenhof. After they did their work, they would bring the body back. They would also hang a wreath on the door, so everyone knew the family was grieving.

My first memory of a funeral is my step-grandmother's, when I was ten or eleven years old. We went up at night to her home; she was lying in the casket, which was placed in the dining room. The table had been moved elsewhere. Other neighbors were also visiting.

Funerals were held at the churches, with the casket brought to the front of the church before going to the cemetery. It was during my early years that the horse-drawn hearse was replaced with an automobile. Sometimes, though, an exception was made for an elderly person who wanted to be taken to their final earthly resting place with the horse-drawn hearse. The horses Mr. Campbell used were solid black.

An example of a metal wreath that was placed on homes when someone had passed away.
Photo courtesy of A.J. Neumann and Ken Fry Centrum Foto Studio.

THE WINTER OF 1936

Some people talk about the "good old days." They must not remember the winter of 1935/1936.

This notorious winter was one for the record books in Jackson County. We refer to it as the "Winter of the Big Snow." I was nine years old and working outside every day. And no matter how I dressed, I was always cold; so was my brother, Darryl. I wore stocking caps, including the aviator cap that was popular back then; two pairs of overalls; long underwear; rubber overshoes; mittens; and sweaters. So much clothing I could hardly move.

Although we had harvested plenty of wood, our supply was being depleted too quickly. We still had a good supply of wood in the timber four or five miles north of town, near the Maquoketa River. The wood was down; we just had to get it out of there.

As the winter increased in duration, it became more of a necessity to get the wood home. Once we got the logs to the house, we used the buzz saw to cut them into the proper lengths for stoves.

One cold January day, Dad kept me home from school. The plan was to take the team and bobsled and bring back a load of logs from the woods. He needed my help to lift and load the logs onto the bobsled.

Because the snow was so deep, the removal equipment of the day was not able to keep the roads open. Fences were cut so people could maneuver their form of transportation—either a car or a horse-drawn bobsled—to where the snow was the least deep. Trails weaved from the road back to the field, depending on the snow cover.

It was really cold in the timber. After Dad tied up the team, he started a fire with the brush that was readily available. In between loading long timber limbs on the sled, we stood by that fire to warm up.

But there is a common problem with brush fires: You roast on one side while the other side freezes.

About noon we started back home. The cold had penetrated deep, and I think the temperature was below zero. I just couldn't get warm. I was shivering so much I finally told my dad I was too cold to keep going.

He said, "You get off the sled and go to the back. Grab the end of a limb and walk. I will keep an eye on you as you trail along."

That helped some, but I just couldn't warm up.

When I got home and took off my shoes and overshoes, I was allowed to put my feet in the oven of the cook stove.

Once I was thawed, there were still the outside chores to do, including milking. Most of the time I didn't like to milk. We sat on a little stool to do the job by hand. But in the winter, I didn't mind milking as much. The barn was always warm because the stock had to stay inside.

DEPRESSION-ERA TRANSPORTATION

Darryl and I rode horses and ponies all the time for pleasure and transportation. Our sister, Shirley, was the horsewoman of the girls. She loved to ride. Her favorite horse was named Topsy.

Topsy was trained to be a rodeo horse. One time, when the rodeo came to Maquoketa, Dad and some other men went to the show. When Dad came home, Topsy was with him. The trainer had told him the only problem this horse had was that a man could not ride her.

Shirley said no problem; she would ride Topsy.

But Dad was determined to ride Topsy, too. Each day he lathered kindness on her, feeding her grain, tickling her behind the ears, and talking to her. One day, he attempted to ride. Topsy was fine with him putting a saddle on, but when he sat in it the poor horse began sweating, shaking uncontrollably, and stomping around. Dad dismounted and never attempted to ride Topsy again.

My dad taught me many things, including how to care for horses. This is him with his favorite team, Bob and Archie.

WHY WOULD YOU WANT A BICYCLE?

So yes, we usually got around on horses. But one week, Darryl and I stayed with an aunt and uncle who lived near Davenport. This aunt was Dad's sister. They had three girls and one boy.

And…they had a bicycle! Bicycles were the newest and latest craze for the girls, who were all riding them.

Darryl and I learned to ride a bicycle during that visit. When we got home, we begged our father for one. I can still hear his reply.

"What do you want a bicycle for?" he bluntly asked, questioning our sanity. "Appears to me you just run your legs off to give your rear end a ride. Makes no sense to me. Just let the horse do the work."

Eventually, we found an old bike and bought it ourselves. From then on, the family had bicycles for the younger brothers and sisters to ride, though Darryl and I still had our horses.

MY FIRST PONY

According to my dad's definition, a pony could be any horse up to 800 pounds that was broken to drive or ride.

I will never forget my first pony, Patches.

Patches was black and white. He had foundered before we purchased him, so he always needed to have his feet trimmed and shod more often than is normal for a horse.

One night after supper, my father gave me a dollar and told me to take Patches to the blacksmith to have shoes put on. He sternly reminded me not to lose the money.

The next morning, I took my pony and money to the blacksmith. It was my first visit to such a place of business. I wasn't sure what to expect when I entered the building. Once my eyes grew accustomed to the darkness, I couldn't help but notice the fire in the forge.

There were several men sitting around the forge, talking and chewing tobacco with an occasional spit. I felt their eyes staring at me and knew they were talking about me. I was a bit intimidated... well, *scared* would be more accurate.

The blacksmith, Mr. Hungerford, was a large man who wore the protective apron that all blacksmiths wore at the time. His features were blackened from the smoke coming from the forge where he was working.

"What do you want, kid?" asked Mr. Hungerford.

"I'm to have my pony's feet trimmed and shod," I answered.

Mr. Hungerford pointed to the sign on the wall: *In God We Trust, All Others Cash.*

"Do you have a buck, kid?" he asked.

With a shaky hand, I gave him my dollar.

"Bring your pony in," he said.

Once Mr. Hungerford was done, you can believe I left immediately.

That was my first visit to the blacksmith. In the following years, I made many more trips to have my pony's feet shod.

THERE'S A CHANGE IN THE AIR

We had food and clothing. Life was good!

But one Sunday afternoon in December, Darryl and I went off hunting rabbit and quail. A little fresh snow was on the ground, which makes for good hunting. It was dusk when we got home. We were doing chores when a bachelor neighbor came to the yard to tell us to turn the radio on—our means of obtaining current news. The Japanese had bombed Pearl Harbor. We all knew we would be in a war soon.

CHAPTER FIVE

Neighbors

During the summer, we relaxed on the porch when the day's work was finished. Neighbors would often stop to chat for a while. If their children were along, we would disappear to play tag, hide-and-go-seek, or ante over. We caught fireflies and played with our homemade rubber guns. Whenever anyone made ice cream it was real treat—it didn't matter the season.

Our neighbors were our friends. They helped us during difficult times.

DOC ROACH

Dr. Roach lived just two doors north from us. He was Preston's veterinarian, and he often wore a suit when making farm calls.

Darryl and I frequently rode along with Dr. Roach to open and close gates for him. That earned us a quarter, which was big money in those days. I always liked animals, and it was interesting for me to see how Dr. Roach practiced his veterinary skills.

When Dr. Roach graduated from the Chicago School of Comparative Medicine in 1900, it was an institution where almost all the professors were physicians. However, they taught both human and veterinary medicine to all their students. Upon graduation, students decided which field to enter.

Dr. Roach chose to be a veterinarian. Yet the Neumann family and many other Preston residents often consulted him for human medical advice as well. If someone in the family had a bad cold, Mother would sometimes call Dr. Roach; he'd often say he would be right over.

"Nettie, you better do this or that," he would say. He would also tell you if he thought you had better see a regular human physician.

One time, one of my sisters was hurt really bad when a play rake accidentally hit her in the head, leaving a deep cut on her forehead. She was bleeding profusely from the wound. Mother called on Dr. Roach, who came right over and stitched her up.

MRS. ROACH

The Roaches subscribed to newspapers and magazines, which they shared with our family once they were finished with them. They also had a set of encyclopedias that they allowed us to use when we had papers to write for school. We would walk over to their home to work on our assignments, using these encyclopedias and the other reference books they had.

Mrs. Roach was a heavy woman. She didn't leave her home much, but she had a passion for playing cards. Before we even had a telephone, she found a way to contact my mother and ask her to send someone over to play cards. Many times, my older sister, Marjorie, and I would go over there and play 500 Rummy—the game Mrs. Roach liked best.

Sometimes I went by myself. There were usually other things I wanted to be doing, but I went where my mother sent me.

I still don't like playing cards.

DOCTORS AND DENTIST

The town always had a doctor, and most set up their offices in their homes. The one exception was Dr. Miller. He had an office uptown.

The dentist, Dr. Glew, had his office in his house. I don't know how my parents did it, but they somehow always managed to have enough money for our annual visit to the dentist. It is possible I still have some of the fillings Dr. Glew put in. He never used Novocain on me.

We always brushed our teeth. Baking soda and toothpaste were our preferred choices, but if we ran out we used lye soap. It didn't matter if the lye soap was homemade or purchased; it rinsed out our mouths real good.

MAE TOMPKINS

Our neighbor, Mae Tompkins, was a spinster who lived with her aged mother. Our family's large garden sat between our two homes. Miss Tompkins came over to help my mother whenever a Neumann child was born. She was there during the birthing and would help my mother around the house during the first days after a new baby was born.

One day, she needed our help—mine especially, since I was the oldest boy.

As usual, I had walked home from school for dinner. It seems Mae Tompkins had noticed a skunk going in and out of her wood shed. She set a trap and had barely caught the skunk by its claws. Using a long bamboo fishing pole, she had managed to drop a washtub—the one that hung on the side of the shed—on top of the skunk, securely trapping it.

Mae asked my mother if one of the boys could come over to shoot the skunk. Mother gave me the shotgun and one shell. She warned me to shoot the skunk in the head, so it wouldn't have a chance to spray. If only wounded, the skunk might utilize his weapon…and then we'd have a stinking mess.

Darryl went with me. Mae Tompkins said she would use the old bamboo fishing pole to lift the tub. She warned me the skunk was loose in the tub and would run off immediately. Her advice was to let it run a ways before shooting it.

I will admit to having been a little bit scared. I may have also been shaking just a mite. The shotgun was a larger gun than I was used to, and the consequence of being sprayed loomed large in my mind.

Mae Tompkins slowly lifted the washtub. I prepared to shoot. The skunk...well, instead of running away it took a few steps and stopped. We had a short standoff, the skunk versus me. I decided to shoot. That didn't go as planned. I missed the skunk; the washtub now featured a big drain hole it didn't have before, and the neighborhood had a new fragrance. And Mae Tompkins was quite angry!

That was not the only time I had a close encounter with a skunk.

Groundhogs[*] like alfalfa. They would ruin fields with the holes they dug, so one day my father sent me out to trap the animals. I placed two traps in a den hole along a creek bank—one at the base and one in another hole at the top of the den. The next morning, I went to check on the traps. The bottom trap had been sprung, but it was empty.

In my excitement, I forgot to glance at the trap above. When I did look up, I was face to face with the rear end of a big old skunk with its tail up. Now, this fellow wasn't too happy and let me have it at full force, in close proximity.

I was sick and vomiting. The spray affected my eyesight. As I got closer to home, the strong smell gave my mother warning. She stopped me before I reached the house and sent me to the wood shed to undress while she heated up some water on the stove top for a bath.

Despite her best efforts, she could not get rid of the smell. She talked to Mae Tompkins, who suggested bathing in tomato juice.

---

[*] *We called them groundhogs, but the more appropriate name is woodchuck.*

Mother brought out many jars of her late summer canning of tomato juice and poured them into the water. It worked, and after rinsing off I was sparkling clean and smelling fresh.

But my clothes…what to do with them? Throwing them away was not an option. Clothing was mighty precious in those days; one didn't just throw clothes away. Mae Tompkins came to the rescue again when she suggested digging a hole and burying the clothes and shoes about two feet underground. We were to keep the soil moist for two weeks, which we did. The two weeks passed, and we dug up the clothing and shoes. *Voilà!* The skunk smell had disappeared.

In later years, whenever we Neumann children came home, Dr. Roach and Mae Tompkins always stopped by to see us. We were happy to have them visit.

JOHANNES MOELLENHOF

Johannes Moellenhof was another neighbor who would stop in whenever he heard the Neumann boys were back home. We called him "Hannes." He always wore leather boots up to his knees. He had white hair and a white mustache, and he was short in stature. He was a good man.

One night, after we had borrowed Mr. Moellenhof's team, we brought them back to his barn. Darryl and I fed and bedded the horses with a foot and a half of straw. We hung the harnesses up before starting our walk home.

"You boys come back here," Mr. Moellenhof hollered in his strong German accent.

We looked at each other and thought, *Oh no, what did we do wrong?* We cautiously entered the barn.

"You see these horses?" he said. "By jiminy, you strawed them up real good. Up to the belly, like it should be done. The horses have worked hard; they need good care. You did that."

CHAPTER SIX

Adventurous, Mischievous, or Just Plain Naughty…

When we had a free moment from work, we played. But our play time also followed the main rule of the Depression: Make do with what you had. Sometimes this led to very unexpected adventures. It's a miracle I survived childhood.

Bib overalls were the uniform of the day. The good pair for school, the patched and repatched pair for work or play.

DAD'S FAVORITE ROOSTER

Our dad had a favorite Black Jersey Giant rooster. It was huge—his pride and joy.

One day, Darryl and I were shooting pigeons from the haymow door. Pigeons were a menace to farmers. They made barns dirty, polluting hay and livestock feed; so farmers were quite happy when their sons reduced the pigeon population. Pigeons were also good to eat, especially the squabs. When we got a squab (a young pigeon), we always gave it away to people who enjoyed them.

We were lying on the hay, looking out the open door. In the far back of the pasture, we saw the rooster strutting around with a few hens and young chicks.

"Betchya can't hit it," I said to Darryl.

"I am sure I can," he shot back.

"Nope, you can't," I challenged him.

"Watch me," he said.

Darryl lay there for the longest time, pointing the .22 before pulling the trigger.

POP!

Would you believe that rooster fell over dead?

We looked at each other, realizing we had really thrown the fat into the fire; but the damage was done, and now we needed to figure out what to do.

We decided to dig a really deep hole in the cornfield and bury the rooster. We even hitched up the cultivator to the horses and cultivated a few rows of corn to cover up our tracks—especially the spot where we had dug the grave.

It was a few days before Dad asked us if we had seen the rooster.

"No, not lately," we answered. "But we *did* see a fox."

Years went by. It wasn't until Darryl and I returned home from the army that we told our dad what had really happened to his prize rooster.

"I always suspected something," Dad said.

CITY COUSINS

Mother's sister lived about twenty miles away, in Clinton. She was married, and their family consisted of three boys and two girls. They would often visit on Sundays. In the summer, the cousins spent time together playing in the pasture, fishing in the creek, and having picnics. But the boys—Allen, Herbie, and Junior—were city boys, and we knew it. We may have gotten carried away in our fun with them a time or two.

Late one Sunday afternoon, they came to visit before supper. Darryl and I were milking cows. The boys came into the barn. We were dressed in our dirty chore clothes, while they were wearing spotless white shirts and brown shorts.

"How do you get milk from cows?" one of them asked.

"Oh, you gotta pump their tails," Darryl and I answered, winking at each other and trying not to laugh.

Our cousins enthusiastically began pumping the cows' tails, even though the tails were dirty. Some manure got on their formerly pristine clothes.

Then one of the cousins noticed the beehives by the line fence.

"What are those?" he asked, pointing out the open door.

"Beehives," we answered. "The bees are busy making honey."

"Can we watch them make honey?"

"Oh sure," we said. "All you have to do is lift the lid and look inside."

The boys did exactly what we told them to do. Out came the angry bees, stinging their innocent victims.

Well, that time we didn't get a spanking. But we sure got a tongue lashing from Mother. She was really angry. Mother didn't get upset that often, but this time she grabbed us and really read us the Riot Act.

THE SKY LIGHTS UP

Outdoor plumbing was the norm for nearly everyone. My parents had a deluxe-style outhouse. Since my dad was a mason, the interior had been plastered, wall papered, and painted. It had a screen door that in the summer helped keep out the flies and provided ventilation. The outhouse also had three seats, two normal-sized ones and a shorter one for youngsters.

Obviously, every night around bedtime everyone would make a trip to the outhouse. During the winter months, when the sun went down earlier, a lantern provided light for this nightly walk. Darryl and I had been given strict orders *not* to play with the lantern. It was to be lighted in the house, so we had no reason to have any matches in our pockets.

But we had gotten in the habit of playing with matches. At night, while we were in the outhouse, we would experiment with extinguishing the lantern and lighting it up again. We blew the spent matches out before throwing them down the convenient hole.

Well, one night, as we boys were getting ready to go upstairs to bed—oh, it must have been twenty minutes or so after we had returned from our cold walk—Dad said, "My, it is awfully bright outside." He went to the window to investigate.

Suddenly, we heard him yell, "The outhouse is on fire!"

Everyone who was able quickly sprang into action, for the fire not only threatened the outhouse, but also the barn and the hog building. Thankfully, *only* the outhouse perished. Darryl and I were taken to the bedroom and justice was applied to our bottoms.

And we deserved it. We both knew we weren't supposed to play with matches.

But our troubles and punishment did not end with the spanking. An outhouse was rather essential. But it could not be replaced overnight, especially in the middle of winter. A new hole needed to be dug in the frozen ground. Back in the 1930s, your tools for digging consisted of a pickaxe and a shovel—nothing as developed and high-tech as what is available today. Dad had to have help from friends and neighbors.

Until the new outhouse was finished, Mother just went to a neighbor's house when she needed to use a toilet. Dad, Darryl, and I used the barn. My younger sisters and brothers used a chamber pot, which Darryl and I were responsible for emptying and cleaning. It was a long time before that outhouse was rebuilt.

Definitely not soon enough for Darryl and me.

A LARGE FIRECRACKER

The Neumann family always celebrated the Fourth of July with fireworks—Roman candles, sky rockets, caps for toy pistols, and a few firecrackers. All these fireworks were deemed safe and handled with care. The adults shot off the more powerful ones, and neighbors would come over in the evening to watch the show.

Albert, the neighbor boy, was a frequent visitor at our house. We were also often at his home. Somewhere along the way—about 1937 or '38, just before the Fourth of July—he came over to visit. We were casing the place, looking for something to do, when he noticed canisters in the rafters of our garage, which doubled as a tool shed. This building was close to the house; Mother did her laundry there.

"What's that up there?" he asked.

"Oh, just dynamite and black powder," Darryl and I answered.

"What do you use that for?"

"Dad uses dynamite to blow out stumps and gunpowder to split logs."

At that time, dynamite and powder were readily available in hardware stores. It was normal for farmers to have both on hand.

A stick of dynamite looked like a large, red firecracker. Just a half stick would blow a stump out of the ground. Darryl and I had seen it used, so we knew how powerful dynamite could be and had a healthy respect for it. We never touched it.

The black powder, on the other hand, was something we were more familiar with because we often used it in the timber. When Darryl and I would cut down oak trees with Dad, we would use a hand-held auger to bore holes in the logs. The logs were typically around 10 feet long and 2.5 feet in diameter, though some were bigger or smaller. Dad would pour black powder in the newly drilled holes. Then he would put a section of fuse in, long enough so part of it remained outside for lighting. Finally, he would fill the hole with dirt and tamp it tight.

After Dad lit the fuse, we would all hide behind some trees. That was more of a safety measure, since there was seldom any flying debris. The charge would go *bang* and split the log lengthwise. The black powder was loud, but it didn't make nearly as much noise as the dynamite.

"Would black powder make a big firecracker?" Albert asked.

"Sure, the *biggest*," we answered.

"Let's do that then."

We brought a ladder over and took down the can of black powder, which had been strategically placed out of our reach. (Darryl and I knew we were not supposed to be messing around with the black powder, but we wanted to build that firecracker.) Our plans got even better when we found a complete roll of Mule-Hide roofing paper. It was in perfect shape for our project.

We were quite clever and industrious, mixing up some cement, which was stuffed into one-third of the Mule-Hide tube. Then, we took a Wonder Bread sack and filled it with black powder. We attached a long fuse to the powder and put the sack in the tube. We filled the remaining third of the tube with more cement, carefully going around the fuse. It took a few days for the cement to harden.

When it did, it looked as though we boys had successfully made a giant firecracker. Now to find the perfect place to set it off.

We decided to use the creek in our pasture as a testing ground.

We worried a bit that the livestock might investigate the firecracker, so we moved all the cows and horses into a pen by the barn. We then placed the firecracker in the creek, which only had four or five inches of water in it. After the long fuse was lit, we all took off running for the hog shed. We planned to watch the explosion from its roof.

The little *bang* we expected to hear turned into a massive *BOOM!* We all scrambled off the roof of the hog shed, driven partly by the force of the explosion and partly by fright. My poor mother had been kneading bread by the kitchen window. The blast blew out a windowpane, sending pieces of glass all over her yeasty dough.

Within two minutes, half the town was at the Neumann home.

Needless to say, Darryl and I made another trip to the brass bed. After the spanking, our father had a few words to say.

"I am glad you put the firecracker in the creek," he told us. "It was also good you used a long fuse, so you had time to get to safety."

But it wasn't really a firecracker; we had made a real bomb.

I am not proud of this story, but it played an important role in my life, then and now. It made me see just how kids can get into big trouble. Every time I read in the paper about kids getting hurt playing with fire or guns, I remember this episode in my life. I don't know why the Lord has been so good to me, when other children were not spared from serious injury or death while playing with explosives.

DRUNKEN CHICKENS

Albert was a few years older than me. One afternoon, we were at his home, which was right across the street from us. Albert's parents were gone, and he was supposed to feed the chickens and gather the eggs.

We were perusing the kitchen when we spotted what became the start of our next innocent adventure: a whiskey bottle.

"That's my dad's," said Albert. "We don't touch it!"

Well, one thing led to another, and we boys decided the breadcrumbs his mother wanted fed to the chickens needed some moistening. We brought the breadcrumb-whiskey mixture out to the chicken house, and the hungry chickens immediately gobbled up their dessert.

The big old rooster could hardly stand; he had to spread his wings out to steady himself. He couldn't crow right, and every time he tried he would almost fall over. The other chickens tried to fly up to the roost, only to fall off. We watched those drunken, hyperactive chickens for a half hour or so, but we were back in the house before Albert's parents returned.

HALLOWEEN

Halloween was a time when practically every boy came out and raised Cain. As long as it didn't get too rowdy, our shenanigans were permitted—yet I do wonder how the town's residents put up with the mischief that occurred.

The boys pulled a lot of pranks—like moving livestock, taking apart vehicles and putting them atop buildings, jacking up Model As, and pushing over outhouses. Sometimes, homeowners would set a mean dog near the outhouse or meet you with their shotgun. When that happened, boys were smart enough to just move on.

There was an elderly couple who lived on the edge of town. Ten of us boys were out together one Halloween, and we pushed over their outhouse. The yard light came on and a man stepped outside. Did we ever light out of there fast! We stopped under a street light in town to catch our breath and talk.

It soon dawned on us that we were missing one of our comrades. We counted again and looked around, but there was no sign of Dizzy (Gerald) Weasmer. We had no idea where he could be, so we waited to see if he'd show up.

After a bit, we heard *slip, slosh, slip—slosh...*

There came Dizzy. He had been near the back corner of the outhouse when we were pushing it over. He slipped and fell into the hole as we were making our escape. It wouldn't have been so bad, but when the yard light came on, he had to crouch down to avoid being seen. He was now a mess.

It was definitely time for a council of war to decide what to do. His mother was a school teacher and his father a mail carrier. His father had a shower in the garage, which helped us out of this predicament tremendously.

We decided some of us would climb the porch into Dizzy's bedroom window to get clean clothes. The rest of us would talk to Mrs. Weasmer while Dizzy showered and our friends retrieved the clothes. We knew Mr. Weasmer was not home.

Knock. Knock.

The door opened.

"Good evening, Mrs. Weasmer," we said politely.

"Why hello, boys," she said.

"Where is Gerald?" we asked.

"He left some time ago," Mrs. Weasmer replied. "I thought he would be with you."

"Nope, we haven't seen him lately," we lied.

"Well, go look for him," she said. "You are sure to find him somewhere."

We kept talking until we were sure everyone else had accomplished their mission. And off we went again.

I have no idea how Dizzy cleaned his clothes and shoes. I am sure he did somehow, because no one threw anything away.

NOT GOOD!

I wasn't part of this prank, and to this day I do not know who was involved.

Some boys got hold of an old cow. They picked the lock of the school and brought it up four flights of stairs to the Assembly Room, where they tied the cow to a desk.

The next morning, Dr. Roach had to be called. The cow would go up the stairs fine, but she would not go down. Dr. Roach gave her a pill to anesthetize her. She was then skidded down the stairs.

People were *not* happy about this incident. School property had been damaged.

AN UNEXPECTED MILK BATH

There was a creamery in town. Across and down the street a ways from the building, there was a row of hitching posts—all that remained from the days when horses were the main source of transportation.

Cream was transported to the creamery in cream cans. Workers would pick up cream cans from farmers every other day with a truck. But on wet days the dirt roads were impassable, so farmers would bring their cream in with horses and a buckboard.

After a can was emptied, it would be set upside down on a rack. Live steam was used to clean and sterilize the can before it was given back to the farmer waiting for it. The scalding water and steam made a bit of noise when they were shot up into the interior of the can. Occasionally, a team of horses would be startled by the noise and take off running.

One day, when I was just a young boy, I was playing in the water in a small ditch. Marjorie, my oldest sister, was nearby on the road, watching me. I heard my mother scream our names. A runaway team of horses with a buckboard was heading directly for us.

When they jumped over the ditch, the milk from the cream cans spilled all over me. They missed my sister and ran around the house. My dad was able to stop the team by the garden.

A RACE WITH A TRAIN

The summer when I was just eleven or twelve years old, I came very close to riding in a hearse.

Johannes Moellenhof had a dairy farm on the southern edge of town. There was a slope down to Main Street from his farm. He also owned or rented some land on the northern side of town. When this land was in hay, he would load the hay on a flat rack and drive it south, up the incline to his farm.

One day, I was helping with his haying operation. All I had to do was drive the team on an empty hay wagon from Mr. Moellenhof's barn on the southern side of town down to the field on the northern side, then take a loaded wagon of loose hay back.

Ol' Hannes was a good horseman, who loved his animals. He had blue roan horses and one team of big black mules. That day, I was driving the span of mules. Everything was going well; I was coming back down the hill with an empty hay rack.

There was a railroad track that ran east and west through town. I had just about gotten to the railroad crossing when here came the local afternoon freight train. It was slowing down, and the engineer was opening the pet cocks of the cylinders on the engine to let the steam fly out. The train was whistling—*pfft, pfft, pfft.*

When the mules heard the noise and saw the steam, they turned and ran along the side of the engine at full speed. The empty wagon, with its steel wheels, was making a lot of noise.

I had absolutely no control of those mules. The depot was coming up; there wasn't enough room in the tight space for the depot, the engine, and the wagon all at one time.

The engineer saw what was happening and was attempting to slow down the engine. The mules and wagon pulled ahead, so I could make it through the narrow opening in the nick of time.

The mules had calmed down by the time we got to the next railroad crossing. They sauntered along as if nothing had happened.

OUR OWN LITTLE CIRCUS

Once a year, the circus came to Maquoketa, the county seat. My parents would load the family up in the back of the red International pickup, and we would take the day off to see the show. Darryl and I would watch the cowboys. One day, we decided we could rope cattle, too.

As children of the Depression years, we were used to making do with what we had. For our roping adventure, we made a lariat out of clothesline. Our intended prey was a younger calf. Because we always rode bareback, we had no saddle to tie the rope to. But we couldn't let that little thing stop us from pursuing our rodeo careers!

We decided to tie the rope around the pony's neck. We rousted all the cattle out of the pen, except for the calf. Riding my pony, I managed to lasso the calf.

The scared calf led out a loud bawl, which frightened the pony. He reared up, and the calf took off running. To keep from totally suffocating, the pony had to run to keep up with the calf.

I tell you, it was a regular circus until we got everything under control.

I kept practicing my roping. I never did become real accomplished at it, but the skill was a necessity when I began my veterinary practice.

CHAPTER SEVEN

High School

The 1940s brought many changes to our family. The Depression was ending. After my step-grandmother passed away, we moved into the house my grandfather Friedrich Neumann had built. Then, the threat of war became a reality when Pearl Harbor was bombed on December 7, 1941.

A NEW HOME

When we moved in 1942, we took the horses and one cow with us. This house my grandfather had built was much more modern. It had electricity, indoor plumbing, and a furnace. However, my dad still used the outhouse. It just didn't seem proper to him to have a bathroom indoors.

The furnace burned wood while Darryl and I were home to cut it. Once we left, Dad started using coal.

There was a summer kitchen attached to the house, where my mother did her canning on the wood-burning stove. A more modern gas stove, a Pyrofax, made life a bit easier for her when she was in the kitchen.

The house Grandfather Neumann built.

MY FIRST SOLO PLASTER JOB

Somewhere about this time, my dad taught me there was more to doing a job than just getting it done.

He took me out to the country to plaster a closet ceiling in a farm house. The ceiling had had its first coat of plaster, or rough coat. It needed a second coat. My dad helped me set up sawhorses and planks I could stand on while I worked.

Then he left.

I worked hard and thought I had done a pretty good job. But when my dad returned in about an hour, he looked at the ceiling and said, "Give me the trowel." He then scraped the new coat of plaster off.

"I will come back in an hour," he said. "You better get it right this time."

I did it over, spending more time putting the plaster on smoothly and evenly. This time my dad was pleased.

There is a difference between doing a job and doing a *good* job. Any profession or work we do well is an art. My dad was an artist with stone. He taught us kids to follow his example.

Fred Vande Weerd knew this, too. He laid the bricks on the house I currently live in. One day, when the house was still under construction, he started on the south wall of the kitchen. The next morning, he was back, undoing the work he had done.

"What are you doing?" I asked him.

"These bricks are not laying perfect," he told me. "And it isn't costing you anything."

That's the same lesson my dad was trying to teach me with my first solo plaster job.

German people like my Grandfather Neumann and my great-uncle—who were, respectively, a captain in the Prussian cavalry and a furrier—have a work ethic they apply to everything: Do good work, be on time, and do not bellyache. Always do a day's work for a day's pay.

A RABID DOG

The school was only two blocks from our new house, and we always went home for lunch. Usually, things were pretty quiet in the neighborhood. One warm day, as we were walking home for dinner, we saw painters working on a house near the school building.

It was such a nice spring day that Mother had left the doors open to let in fresh air, including the screen door on the kitchen.

We were eating our lunch when, all of a sudden, a dog came running toward the house at full speed. He came right inside through the open screen door and raced through the kitchen, bursting into the dining room.

The dog was drooling, and when my mother saw the white foam she yelled, *"Rabies!"*

Now let me tell you, polio and rabies were two of the biggest fears we children had while growing up because there was no cure.

So we all jumped on top of the table. The dishes went flying, the dog ran in a circle in the dining room, through the living room, and right into my parents' bedroom, where he took refuge under the bed.

My mother swiftly ran over and shut the bedroom door. Then she called Dr. Roach.

"You have to come right away," she said in a highly excited voice. "There is a rabid dog in my house, hiding under my bed."

While we were cleaning up the broken dishes, Dr. Roach came in.

"Where is the dog?" he asked.

"In the bedroom, over there," Mother answered.

Dr. Roach was a portly man. He cautiously opened the door to peer inside.

"Nettie," he said. "I think I smell the cause of this dog's problem."

He got down on his hands and knees to approach the dog, who was lying under the bed, shaking.

"He doesn't have rabies," said Dr. Roach. "I can smell turpentine."

We soon found out the painters had been bothered by this dog. When they could no longer put up with it, they proceeded to turpentine it.

My mother lost some of her dishes. To this day, I can't figure out how all seven of us kids got on that little table.

WAR DRIVES

World War II had begun, as so many people had predicted. Like many high school students of the day, I was involved in drives for bonds. I also participated in the many drives for scrap iron, copper, and other metals. Brass, iron, copper, and antique car parts were given a new purpose. A favorite place of ours to hunt for the needed material was a vacated dump near town that was partially covered with dirt.

Rationing affected us, particularly flour rationing since Mother did a lot of baking. Our neighbor, Mrs. Roach, didn't use all her sugar, so she would share those ration coupons with us. Shoes and clothing were patched and patched again because there wasn't much new material available.

Cars and machinery were scarce in those years, so horses stayed in vogue. Tires on Model A and Model T cars were worn smooth. The horse-hide robes every farmer kept for bobsled rides were used inside cars for warmth. When a car was parked by the curb in town, the robes were thrown over the car engine to keep the radiator warm.

The rationing of gasoline and tires was one more thing we high school students had to prepare for when planning our senior class trip. We had to pool together gasoline coupons for the day's excursion. Our class of fourteen went to a bowling alley in Maquoketa, where I bowled my first game. We also enjoyed a paddle-wheeled steamboat ride on the Mississippi River.

Patriotic programs were also common. They usually advertised the sale of some product to be sent to the armed forces. Women held sewing bees and knitted scarves and socks. They also sent food items. Candy was a popular item to send, as it wouldn't perish. The food would be collected at a specific gathering point, and then the women worked together to pack the boxes for the soldiers. They also wrote letters to servicemen.

Others volunteered to work at the hospital in Clinton. Some worked across the Mississippi River, making ammunition at the Savanna Proving Grounds in Illinois.

The war affected us all.

MASS COMMUNICATION

When we went to the movies, the newsreels that preceded each film kept us informed about the fighting and the war. Another news source was the *Clinton Herald*, a daily newspaper. The Roaches received the Sunday *Des Moines Register*, which they passed to the Neumann family when they were done reading it.

And the Zenith radio! Our family gathered around it each evening.

Boxing was popular, especially with menfolk. Their big thing to listen to was boxing matches between famous athletes, like Joe Lewis and Max Schmeling. Many men would listen to the radio at night between eight and nine o'clock to cheer on their favorite boxer.

Everyone worked hard to see that the crops were planted and harvested.

U.S. NAVY-TEST-V-12

I was just sixteen when I graduated from high school in 1943. My seventeenth birthday was a month later. I wanted to enlist, but I was too young and my parents would not sign the papers.

During my last month of high school, I heard of the U.S. Navy-Test-V-12 program. Those accepted would be trained as aviators, with the goal of becoming navy pilots. I had in my mind that I wanted to be a torpedo bomber, which was probably a very dangerous position.

I took the written test under supervision at school. It was sent off to Des Moines. I passed and received notice to appear in Des Moines for a physical. If I passed the physical, I could enroll in the naval program.

Des Moines was a big city, bigger than any place I had ever been to before. My older sister, Marjorie, went along. I passed, but I was a half-inch too short. The navy chief said that wasn't a problem; he pointed to a rod I could hang from for an hour or so. Then they would measure me again. So I hung there for an hour, but I still came up too short. They wouldn't take me.

World War II loomed large as we considered our future plans.

I am the first boy on the left in the back row, next to my brother Darryl. The Preston High School team was champion of Jackson County in 1943.

CHAPTER EIGHT

Off to College

When the U.S. Navy program would not accept me, I had a "now-what-do-I-do" moment. My parents really wanted me to go to college, since I had graduated top of my high school class. They told me that while they had very little money, they would help me pay for my schooling as much as they could.

Because of my association with Dr. Roach, I had always wanted to be a veterinarian. But that wasn't a simple decision to make, since Dr. Roach thought I would make a good surgeon. He told me that if I became a surgeon, he would pay for my education. But I ultimately decided to stay with my plan to become an animal doctor.

ROOM AND BOARD

I enrolled at Iowa State. Because the war was going on, the college held classes year-round. Dr. Roach's son, Vincent, lived in Ames; Vincent said I could stay with his family during my first week on campus, while I spent time learning about the college. I worked around the Roaches' home when I was not at school. It was summertime, and there was plenty of gardening and lawn mowing to do.

As I was getting ready to move into a dorm room, the Roaches offered to provide me with a room in exchange for labor. Vincent worked for General Filter Company, which kept him busy; he was often away from home. The family had an upstairs bedroom where I could study and sleep. This arrangement was agreeable to me, since I wouldn't have the expense of a dorm room.

The Roaches' home was about a mile from the college. Every day, rain or shine, I walked under the sycamore trees along the Cinder Path to the campus. For a time, I did try bicycling, but it was more work than it was worth. Bicycles were stolen if they weren't padlocked, and I had to transport my books. The Cinder Path was a walking path used by pedestrians and bicyclists. It went from the western edge of Ames to the college. As its name implies, it was covered with cinders—the all-weather path surface. I crossed the same bridge over Squaw Creek that the trains crossed.

I studied at night, since there was very little time in between classes for it. I had a manual typewriter. Even though I was a fairly good typist in school, too often I found myself using the hunt-and-peck system. I also had a bottle of ink on my desk that I filled my pens with. Sheaffer pens—manufactured in Fort Madison, Iowa[*]—were in their glory days. Ballpoint pens were not yet popular.

Each week, I would send my laundry home to my mother. Since most students did that, there were actual laundry boxes designed for the task. The laundry boxes would shut tight with canvas straps, and there was a place to slip in the address. Once cleaned, my mother would send the laundry back. She'd press it, too, using a mangle iron.

The boarding arrangement provided a place for me to sleep and study. To save money during my first year, I only ate one meal a day. I usually walked three blocks from the college to a restaurant.

There is a Sheaffer Pen Museum in Fort Madison.

Somehow, this got back to the Roaches, who reconsidered our agreement. They included meals the next year. If that had not happened, I don't know if I would have continued with college.

I did a lot of work for my room and board: painting the house inside and out, varnishing the woodwork, shingling the roof, gardening, stoking and caring for the coal furnace, mowing the lawn, removing snow in the winter, and babysitting their three young children—something I had plenty of practice with.

THE CLASS OF '49

My education got off to a good start, but it was interrupted when I received my draft notice in 1945. I had only eight quarters remaining when I exchanged college life for military service. The war soon ended; twelve months later, I resumed my college education exactly where it had been interrupted. That's how it worked. Veterans were able to just step back into their academic careers.

Almost every man in my class of sixty-five students was a veteran. One man had been a colonel in the army's cavalry. One short fellow had been a commander on an aircraft carrier. Many of the men were older and had wives, who had jobs. I and one other man were the youngest in the group. There was one girl who started with the class, but she later quit.

Some of my classmates became famous in their fields. Dr. T.J. Lafeber focused his veterinary practice on avian medicine. He became well-known in the field and founded Lafeber Company, which sold bird food from formulas he developed. Another classmate went to Kentucky and became celebrated in thoroughbred racing.

The class of '49 scattered all over. We held our last class reunion—our fiftieth—in 1999. Now, twenty years since that reunion, almost everyone has passed away.

CODES OF CONDUCT

The majority of our instructors were older men who had started their teaching careers prior to World War II. There was a dress code everyone adhered to: shirt, tie, and trousers. Definitely no shorts. It was okay to wear military clothing. The professors wanted us to look professional, neat, and clean—not sloppy.

There was also a code of conduct. Anyone caught cheating would not be let back in. Tardiness and excuses for missing classes were discouraged.

I had really good instructors. Years later, I visited the college to talk to one of them, Dr. Emerson. This man was a tough professor who taught obstetrics. He did not hand out A's easily. If a student received one, they really earned it. I was one of the few students who did earn an A.

I waited until his class was over before making my presence known.

"Did you see that mob?" asked Dr. Emerson.

"Yes, I did," I answered.

"It *is* a mob," said Dr. Emerson. "I sure do wish we had that dress code back."

ENGINEERS VS. VETERINARIANS

There was a bit of rivalry between the engineering and veterinary students. When the engineers had lectures over in the veterinary department, they would mix up chemicals and dot the terrazzo floors with the solution. When anyone stepped on it, there would be a big bang that scared the living daylights out of the victim.

One day, we decided to get our revenge. We went down to the anatomy room and cut parts off the dead animals stored there. While the engineers were attending their lecture, we slipped these "gifts" into their coat pockets.

The next thing we knew, there was a special meeting called for the veterinary students. All the heads of the departments were there…and they were absolutely furious.

It seems those coats did not belong to the engineering students. Rather, the governor of Iowa and members of the State Board of Education had been meeting in the lecture room. Talk about *trouble*.

The deans wanted to know who was responsible. That person would be expelled. Not a soul spoke. It was as if no one knew anything about the situation.

Thank the Lord the students had been military personnel. They knew how to keep their mouths shut in tough spots.

In time, the trouble passed over.

CHRISTMAS CHEMISTRY

Some of the veterinary students took an elective chemistry class in the home economics department. It was taught by a husband and wife, who were graduate students. The class also included many girls.

The class finished at the end of the term, which coincided with Christmas break. We decided to have a party to celebrate the holiday. The instructors made homemade treats, including popcorn balls of different colors. I chose a green one; most of us ate our popcorn balls at the party.

Later, when I went to the bathroom, my urine was green. I and the men knew what had happened, but some of the girls panicked and hurried to the ER at the hospital.

SUMMER WORK

After the war, the college went back to having summers off. The summer between my sophomore and junior year was a scorcher. I joined Darryl, who was home from his paratrooper service, and together we helped Dad with his masonry business.

That summer we built a house for Bill Hass right next to our parents' home. It was built over our old potato garden and was the last house in Preston to have its basement dug with a slip scraper and team of horses. Because of the heat, we adjusted our schedule to work during the night using electric lighting.

The next summer, I took on a very challenging job. Looking back, I wonder how I ever thought I could do it and why anyone trusted me with it.

General Filter Company wanted a warehouse built. According to the job description, the contractor would need to construct a building complete with a floor and trusses in place for the roof.

I applied and was awarded the bid. I hired a mason, the mason's father, and an old, decrepit carpenter. We had twelve weeks to complete the job. We did it in six, working long hours each day without any big machinery.

When I finished, I had $1,000 in my pocket. I was on top of the world. This was enough money to purchase a $400 used car from my uncle and aunt, who ran a Ford dealership. I could also buy the instruments I needed to start my veterinary practice. Both were necessary to beginning my career.

Best of all, there was no debt!

True, the GI Bill paid for my tuition and books. I also worked for my room and board, so I saved money there. I didn't spend money on frills. I didn't date or go out. While working in the Roaches' garden during the fall, I could hear the cheers from people enjoying the nearby football game.

Some people tell me they wouldn't go to college if they had to go the way I did. But college is an investment. If you want to continue your education, you must be prepared to work hard to pay for it.

CHAPTER NINE

Off to the Military

I was drafted in early 1945. On July 27, I was sworn into the army at the Jefferson Barracks Military Post near St. Louis, Missouri.

It was a raucous trip from Ames to Jefferson Barracks, the oldest operational military post west of the Mississippi. It was originally established in 1826 as the country's first Infantry School of Practice. In late April, Germany had capitulated; the men were jubilant, as the end of the war was in sight. I remember some of them removing the train car chairs and tossing them out the windows. No one attempted to stop them.

FIRST NIGHT IN THE BARRACKS

That first night, the sergeant came into the barracks at nine o'clock and ordered the lights out. We were to stay in the sack until he returned in the morning.

The barracks were a filthy mess. Pretty soon, we heard a lot of little scratching noises. We turned our flashlights on, only to see that the place was crawling with cockroaches, which were investigating the paper wrappers on the floor.

BECOMING A MEDIC

I was soon sent to Camp Crowder—near Neosho, Missouri, close to the Arkansas border. It was there that I completed my basic training. There were some in the company who had never handled a gun before. My hunting background helped me excel in the use of small arms.

From there, I was sent to Columbia, South Carolina, where I was put on notice that I would be shipped overseas. This was a time filled with uncertainty. We were often commanded to be ready to leave, only to have the orders cancelled. Since World War II was almost over, infantry soldiers were no longer in demand.

When the army decided I should serve as a medic, I was put on a troop train en route to Fitzsimons General Hospital in Denver, Colorado. This was not a luxury sightseeing train. It was hot and unairconditioned. The meals were served on an open car. If the wind was right, the smoke and cinders from the engine would fly over us, forcing us to take our food back inside.

The train stopped in North Platte, Nebraska. We all got off and marched down to the city park. A group of ladies gave us a wonderful home-cooked meal—fried chicken and all the fixings. That meant a lot to us.

The train dropped some of us off at the depot in Denver, where we were transferred to the hospital. In later years, whenever I flew into Denver's old airport, this hospital was one of the landmarks I recognized. My training there prepared me to be a surgical technician.

Thanksgiving at the hospital was quite memorable; we all got really sick from food poisoning.

CAMP CARSON

Christmas was a whole lot better. By then, I was working at Camp Carson, near Colorado Springs. Here I worked in the German POW wards, where German prisoners sent to the United States provided labor on some farms.

It was the best job I had in the army. These men were plain, ordinary soldiers. I could understand some of their native language. They could also communicate in English.

When I looked outside on Christmas Day, I saw there was just a skiff of snow on the ground. All of a sudden, I heard a commotion in the twenty-bed ward. The men were looking out a window, shouting, *"Hase."* When I went to look, I saw they were excited about seeing a large jackrabbit.

When the hospital closed its doors, I was sent to Lawson General Hospital in Atlanta, Georgia, where I worked with amputees.

CAPTAIN MANASMITH

In Atlanta, I met a veterinarian—Dr. Manasmith from Red Oak, Iowa—who was a captain in the Army Veterinary Corps. Veterinarians inspected the farms and other food establishments that supplied provisions for the army. They also took care of any horses and other animals on army posts.

Captain Manasmith somehow knew I was a veterinary student from Iowa. He chose me to be his driver and assistant. When he had inspections to do, on or off the post, I would go down to the motor pool to pick up a jeep.

He mostly inspected mess halls and food supplies. Once, he inspected a Coca-Cola plant in Atlanta that was supplying the army with their products.

Occasionally, Captain Manasmith would send me to inspect a mess hall. I often wondered what those big, burly chefs thought about little ol' me doing these inspections.

TRANSPORTING THOSE RELEASED FROM THE HOSPITAL

If we were selected for a certain work detail, the information was posted on the company bulletin board.

One time, I accompanied a black serviceman who was going home from the hospital. My responsibility was to take care of his needs and luggage. We went by train to Tuskegee, Alabama. A military vehicle then took us to the army airfield that, at the time, only trained black servicemen.

I stood at attention while the officer in charge went through our papers and began his interrogation.

"Did you have a good trip?" he asked the serviceman.

"Yes, sir," the man answered.

"Were you well taken care of?"

"Yes, sir."

When all was squared away, I was discharged. He informed me that I had ten minutes to leave the post.

"Sir, I have not eaten since yesterday," I said.

"You have ten minutes to leave the post," he repeated.

I was escorted out the door. There was a woman waiting for me. Her job was to see that I got onto a military vehicle that would take me to the railroad station in Tuskegee.

Since I was hungry, after arriving at the station I wandered over to the general store. In there, I noticed footprints painted on the floor. Directly ahead of the footprints was an open Bible. A nearby sign read, "If you can read these words in the Bible, you do not need glasses."

Three black college students came up to me.

"Did you just come from the military post?" they asked.

"Yes, I did," I replied.

"Would you like to see the college and the museum?"

"Sure, I would."

My tour guides were very nice to me. They bought me breakfast before we spent the rest of my free time seeing the town, which included the Tuskegee Institute founded by Booker T. Washington. George Washington Carver had been an instructor there. Before teaching at Tuskegee, Carver had graduated from Iowa State and been on the faculty there. He went on to develop many new uses for crops, especially peanuts.

WEEKEND PASSES

Occasionally, we were given weekend passes; but I was too far from home to make a trip there. I had become friends with Jack London, a married veterinarian. One time, when we both had passes on the same weekend, he invited me to come home with him.

"We have plenty of room," said Jack. "So come along with me to Goodwater, Alabama. By the way…have you ever eaten frog legs?"

"No, I have not," I replied.

"Well, then you got to come," he insisted. "We will go frog-gigging."

I couldn't resist an invitation like that. He wasn't kidding when he said they had plenty of room. Their home was a giant, two-story Southern house. His wife was living with his parents while he was in the service.

That first night we went out frog-gigging. With a long spear and a flashlight, we hunted great, big bullfrogs. When we caught one, we threw it into a burlap sack. Jack London's mother cooked it for dinner.

"Where did you get this?" she asked. "I hope you didn't go by the dam. It's full of snakes."

That is exactly where we had gone. If I had known that, I would not have been so excited about frog-gigging.

I knew Jack London's grandfather lived upstairs and would join the family for supper. He didn't show up the first night when I was there. But the second night, the Confederate Army veteran ate with us. I asked my friend about it.

"He didn't want to eat with a Yankee," Jack answered. "But when he found out you were from Iowa, and not out east, he figured you were not a Blue-Belly Yankee. So, it was okay to eat with you."

I enjoyed this family's hospitality twice before being transferred to the Percy Jones General Hospital in Battle Creek, Michigan. It was a military hospital that had all kinds of patients. I did general work in the wards under the direction of the nurse in charge.

It was there that I received my discharge orders. I returned to Iowa State to pick up where I had left off in my studies.

We finished our basics at Camp Crowder in Missouri.

Mr. Nye of Louisiana and I were young men when we took basic training together.

Darryl and I, my best friend and brother. He was a paratrooper with the 81st Airborne Unit during WWII.

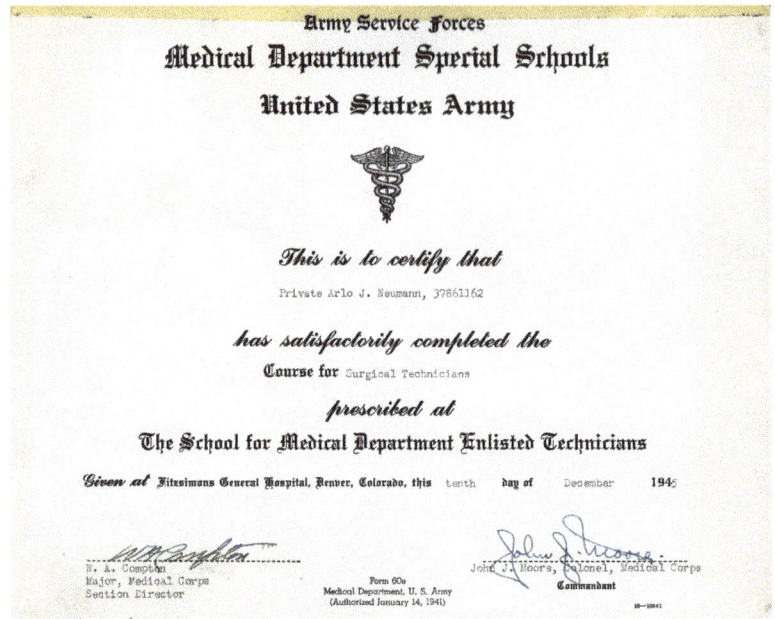

At the Fitzsimons General Hospital, I earned my surgical technician's certificate.

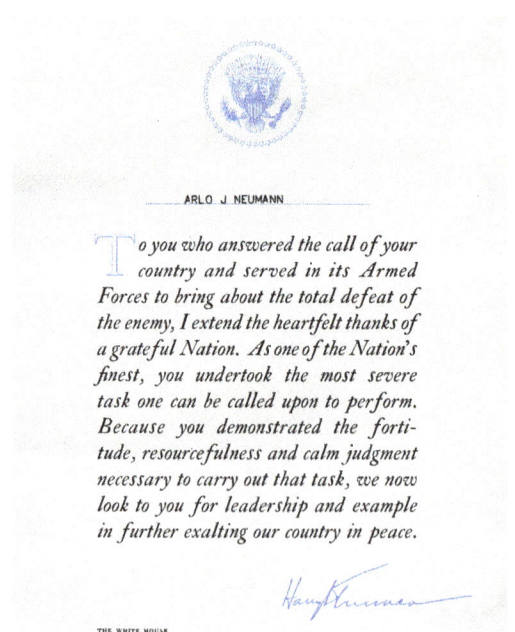

A thank-you from President Harry S. Truman.

PART II

The Clinic Years

CHAPTER TEN

You Are Moving Where? Never Heard of That Town.

Toward the end of my senior year, everyone was talking about their jobs. Some were investigating prospects, while others already knew where they were going to work. A few of us—including me—were just plain looking. A veterinary job was not that easy to come by.

Then one day, I was called into the Dean's office. Two men from Orange City were there: Robert Fisher, D.V.M., and Teunis E. Klay, or "Deacon Klay," as he was called. In 1955, Deacon Klay was appointed Iowa District Court Judge. But that was later in his career. Now it was 1949, and he was a lawyer in town.

"These men are looking for a veterinarian who is short, doesn't drink, and doesn't smoke," said the Dean. "And someone who would make a good general practitioner."

I qualified on the first three, and my goal was to be the best veterinarian there could be. Dr. Fisher and Deacon Klay interviewed me, and I made two trips to Orange City to see the town. I had never heard of it before that day in the Dean's office.

VAN DE WAA AND FISHER CLINIC

Everything looked good to me, so I said I would take the job. On June 10, 1949, I arrived in town to work at the Van de Waa and Fisher Clinic. Henry Van de Waa was the son of Hendrik Jan Van de Waa, one of the four men who searched out Sioux County and claimed it as the place for a new colony of American Hollanders from Pella, Iowa. The Van de Waa family farm was just north of Orange City; it was then known as the Art Reekers farm.

Dr. Van de Waa was the second licensed veterinarian in Sioux County. Twenty years before I was born, he began his practice in Orange City. He had died suddenly while vacationing in January 1949. I was to replace him.

His wife, Cornelia "Kitty" (Klein) Van de Waa, was the daughter of John T. Klein and Henrietta (Hospers) Klein. Henrietta was the daughter of Henry and Cornelia Hospers; Mr. Henry Hospers is often referred to as a founding father of Orange City. Their farm was just northwest of Orange City and later became the County Farm.

Cornelia married Edward Fisher in 1912. He was a mail carrier who delivered letters and packages on his motorcycle. His brother-in-law, Henry Van de Waa, encouraged him to study to be a veterinarian.

Fisher took his advice, graduating from Iowa State College in 1917. He joined his brother-in-law's clinic, which was renamed Van de Waa and Fisher. When Dr. Ed Fisher developed heart problems in the late 1940s, his son, Robert, joined the clinic. Dr. Robert Fisher had a thriving business in Ireton, but he relocated to Orange City upon his father's request. Most of his clients' business followed him there.

Dr. Ed Fisher still worked in the office, dispensing medicines and answering the telephone. Mrs. Betty Van Marel also worked in the office. Dr. Fisher died on May 4, 1950.

And that's a bit of history of the place where I began working right after I passed my state boards.

The building with the horses in front was the city livery barn where Dr. H.J. Van de Waa first practiced veterinary medicine in Orange City.

This building, which formerly served as the blacksmith shop, was purchased by Drs. Van de Waa and Fisher to be their new veterinary clinic. It was here that I began my practice as an employee of Dr. Robert Fisher.

Photos courtesy of *The Centennial Book: Orange City, Iowa, 1870-1970*, printed by the Ad-Visor. Centennial Book Production Staff: Rev. E. Van Engelenhoven, Editor; Harvey Pluim, Publisher; Edward Stetson, Design; Fred Brandes, Composition; and Keyron Shumacher, Pressman.

AN UNUSUAL WELCOME

When I came to Orange City on Friday, the plan was for me to stay with Dr. Ed and Gertrude Fisher until I could find a more permanent residence. They had a bedroom waiting for me.

Their home was a big, two-story house on the north side of Second Street and Albany. The veterinary clinic was located just west of the house, in a large, old frame building that had once been a blacksmith shop. There was no basement.

Before moving to that location, Van de Waa had had office space in the Skelly Oil Station, located where the Flower Cart is today. The station was owned by Gerrit Van Klompenburg. Jack Ver Steeg worked there and owned a tank wagon for delivering fuel to the country. It's a bit ironic, but the Skelly Station replaced the livery barn in town.

It was about four o'clock in the afternoon when I parked my car in front of the house. I noticed a lady sitting on a bench in the front yard. It was a nice day, so I didn't give it much thought. I got out of my car and was preparing to get my luggage, when all of a sudden that lady jumped up and screamed before starting to cry. She took off running, crossing the street toward the south.

I thought, *What's this?* It was one unusual welcome to a town clear across the state from my home.

Later I learned she was Mrs. Henry Van de Waa, the widow of the man I was replacing. She had been sitting there, waiting to see her husband's replacement. She was shocked when she saw me because I bore a striking resemblance to her husband when they had married.

Farmers often told me I reminded them of Dr. Van de Waa in appearance. When I saw pictures of the man from his youth, I could see the resemblance, too.

MY FIRST FARM CALL

Once my luggage was in my room, I went to the office to report for duty. I was outfitted with some drugs and instruments and sent out on my first call.

The call was three miles west, one south, and then a quarter mile east—Henry Addink's farm.

Henry Addink was tall and built well with a large frame, but he was not heavy. A bull calf had been castrated earlier and was now infected in that area. It was a good first call, the beginning of a friendship that continues to this day.

My starting salary was $250 a month. My gasoline was furnished. I basically worked seven days a week, as emergencies often cropped up on Sundays. Many times, farmers were reluctant to call on Sunday, but when they did it didn't matter their religious affiliation. They respected the Fourth Commandment, given in Exodus 20: 8-11:

> *Remember the sabbath day, to keep it holy. Six days shalt thou labour, and do all thy work: but the seventh day is the sabbath of the Lord thy God: in it thou shalt not do any work, thou, nor thy son, nor thy daughter, thy manservant, nor thy maidservant, nor thy cattle, nor thy stranger that is within thy gates: for in six days the Lord made heaven and earth, the sea, and all that in them is, and rested the seventh day: wherefore the Lord blessed the sabbath day, and hallowed it.*

Farmers back then usually paid for the farm calls immediately, but they deferred on Sunday. "It is the Lord's Day. I will be in first thing Monday morning to pay you," they said. And they were always there bright and early the next morning.

When I started, almost all the veterinarians in the area were elderly. They all came to the office to personally welcome me to the area. I appreciated it.

One veterinarian in Rock Valley still wore the work attire of his generation: a suit and tie. When they came to a farm, they would take their suit coat and tie off and cover their clothing with a smock. I wore blue jeans and a shirt.

FIRST FRIENDS

I soon found more permanent residence in a home owned by Mr. and Mrs. Mitch Moret. They were a young couple who rented out rooms in the upstairs of their home for sleeping in. She was a school teacher and he worked at Northwestern State Bank.

The rooms were rented out to me; Lloyd Kepp, an architect; and a Northwestern College professor. Because the rooms were just for sleeping, we usually took our evening meal at Albert Grooters' café.

There was a regular group of us who got together to eat, including Lloyd Kepp and his father, Bill. Lloyd's girlfriend, Mary Bakke, also frequently joined us. She was a school teacher in Orange City and later became his wife. The large table along the west side of the café was where our lifelong friendship had its beginnings.

CHAPTER ELEVEN

Who Is That Girl?

My high school class was small. There were only fourteen of us in my grade. The junior class was somewhat larger, but I don't remember by how many students. I know it wasn't many, because there weren't a lot of students in the Preston school system.

It bothered my mother a bit that I didn't go to the junior-senior prom. I helped my dad finish the steps of the Catholic church the night of the dance, and she couldn't understand it. My mom wanted me to associate more with girls, but I was getting along fine without them. In high school, I didn't date at all.

In my college years, I was absolutely broke all the time. I barely had enough money to get along myself. I didn't have time to go to college events because I was always working or studying. After my service in the military during World War II, the GI Bill paid for my books and tuition. But I still didn't participate much in social activities.

I did go out once or twice with a girl from home. She was a real good friend of my brother's wife. Without my knowledge, they arranged for this young lady to come to my graduation. (More on that later.)

My concerns at the time were getting my college studies completed and finishing up on some work at the Roaches' house. I had promised them I would paint some of their interior rooms before I graduated. The kitchen needed the most work.

So college courses, painting, and varnishing the kitchen were the only things on my mind…until one day.

WHO IS THAT GIRL?

There was a paint store in Ames called Irvine Paint and Wallpaper. Mrs. Irvine was active in the Methodist church choir, as was Mr. Roach, who had an exceptional voice. Sometimes Mrs. Roach played the organ during services. Occasionally, I went to the Methodist church with the Roaches on Sunday.

Anyway, I could go to the Irvine store and charge whatever supplies I needed for the Roaches' house. One day, about two-and-a-half months before graduation, I went to the store to get some more paint.

There was this good-looking young gal behind the counter. She took my order and mixed up the paint to the color it needed to be. Then she handed it to me. I was struck. I looked at her and thought, *This is really a lady.*

Later that day I asked Mrs. Roach, "Who was that girl?"

"Oh, that was Mary Virginia Prather," she answered. "She sings in the choir and works for the Irvines almost all the time."

"I would like to take her out," I said.

"Do you want me to ask her?" she offered.

"No, I will ask her," I replied.

The next time I went for painting supplies, I asked Mary if she would like to go out when she had a Saturday night free.

She said she would.

We did the typical college deal: movie, eat somewhere, and go home. There was one thing different. We had to walk. I did have a car, but not enough money for gasoline to put in it. So, it sat at the Roaches' house.

It was quite a walk to the movies and restaurant. The Prathers lived on the north edge of town—in a large, beautiful two-story home at 1528 Grand Avenue.* It was a mile-and-a-half walk from where I lived to their home. Then another three-quarters of a mile to the movie theatre.

Mary and I went out several times. The more I took her out, the more I liked her. Then one day she asked me, "You have a car, don't you?"

"Yes," I answered.

"Then why don't you drive it?"

"I don't have the money for fuel," I said. "I have to use what I've got for graduation and beginning my veterinary job."

"Oh, I have enough money for gasoline," she replied.

So we used the car. All her life, Mary loved to drive.

COLLEGE GRADUATION

Graduation was coming up, and I asked Mary to come. She said she would.

My brother's wife and her friend heard I had asked somebody to go to my graduation. Boy, that didn't go over very well. But I had never made any arrangements with that other girl.

About that time, Dr. Fisher and Deacon Klay came down to the school, looking to replace Dr. Van de Waa. They talked with me at length, and I agreed to look at the job.

Mary came with me for a day trip. We got to see what Orange City looked like and meet a few people. She sat in when Dr. Fisher discussed the job with me. That was our first introduction to the town.

At my graduation ceremony in June, Mary sat with the Neumann family group.

---

* *The big fireplace in the Prather home helped me make a good impression on Mary's family. It was unsafe to use because the fire bricks had burned out. My masonry background came in handy, as I knew how to repair it with fire clay mortar and new fire bricks.*

My mother was extremely proud of my feat. I was the first one of the family to graduate as a professional, which meant a lot to my mother. My dad was also proud. Both my parents had gone to school through the eighth grade and then went off to work. Dad was a vocal proponent of education, though. He often encouraged us to get an education and do better with our lives.

When I brought Mary to see the Tulip Festival in Orange City, she stayed at the Klays' house. She could then see more of the Dutch community and what my practice was like. Deacon and Effie Klay were very good to Mary and me.

When I worked for Dr. Fisher, I would get every other weekend off. As soon as my work was done on Friday or Saturday night, I could leave. I would go to Ames and stay with the Roaches. Mary and I would do something together. We would also spend time with her family. Her dad was the city clerk before he retired. She had three younger brothers: Jack, Jim, and Joe. Jack and Jim were quite reserved. Joe was the youngest, and he was always trying to impress me.

Mary was introduced to all my family on the Fourth of July in 1949. We celebrated the holiday in Bellevue, on the banks of the Mississippi River. She had a good time and met a lot of Neumanns, including my brothers and sisters. She had already met my folks at graduation.

SHE SAID YES!

I just asked her to marry me, and she said yes…but she would have to talk to her dad first.

My salary was $250 a month. The only thing the vet practice supplied me with was the gasoline to put in my car. I had to furnish the vehicle, tires, and repairs. After rent and other living expenses, there wasn't much left over. Somehow I saved enough money to purchase an engagement ring at Gunderson's Jewelry in Sioux City.

We got engaged in 1950…or was it toward the end of '49? If Mary was alive, she would know the exact hour and day. We married in the Methodist church in Ames on November 5, 1950.

At our wedding, the best man was Dr. Carl Van de Waa, the son of the man I was hired to replace. He was a dentist and worked for the veterans' hospital in Sioux Falls. He was a single man and came down every weekend to visit his mother. While there he would ride along on calls, and we hunted during the fall. We became friends, and so he stood up for me at the wedding. Mary had a girlfriend stand up for her.

AN UNUSUAL BUSINESS DEAL

Like most people of that time, we didn't have much money. Mary had saved some from her job at the paint and wallpaper store. I was making payments on my half-interest in the vet practice.

Dr. Fisher had sold me the half-interest in June 1950. He was a wonderful partner. But there probably haven't been many business deals like ours.

We were working on inventory one day. Once we were done, I was to buy half of it as my interest in the practice. We had been working for about ten minutes when Dr. Fisher said to me, "I just want to play golf."

It was his day off, and he usually played with the Thursday Club when he wasn't working. He offered to just quote me a figure. The figure was astonishingly low. I said it was fine, that I would take it. Dr. Fisher then wanted to go to the bank immediately to sign the papers (so he could go play golf). That is exactly what we did. Afterward, I made quarterly payments on the note.

We practiced together fourteen years. I could not have asked for a better partner to work with than Dr. Fisher.

EARLY YEARS IN ORANGE CITY

After we were married, Mary and I rented a small upstairs apartment in town. Some friends of ours lived in the apartment downstairs.

One day, they told us our landlady had been coming in while we were gone and going through our dressers and drawers. We confronted the landlady with this information; it was not the best of scenes. So after six months of living there, we moved into a single room in a big, old house on the south end of Main Street.

I felt this was hard on Mary. Her first few years in Orange City were probably quite challenging. She had less opportunity than I did to meet and mix with the Dutch people on a daily basis. The biggest issue she had was going to the grocery store, because in those days they still spoke a lot of Dutch downtown. In fact, they still spoke Dutch at some of the church services. At the store, she would hear people talking in Dutch. They would look at her, and though she didn't know what they were saying she supposed they were talking about her.

However, the Dutch were overall polite and good to us, especially Mary. Slowly, speaking in Dutch became less common. Time took care of that.

Mary danced in the Tulip Festival in 1951. It was a surprise to me, but she enjoyed being out with people.

KEPP APARTMENTS

We patiently waited for Kepp Construction to finish building their new rental apartment building in town. (The company was owned by my friend, Lloyd Kepp, and his brother, Ward.) When it was complete in late summer 1951, we moved in. They had built a number of very nice apartments. Ours was in the northwest corner of the building. It consisted of a bedroom, bathroom, dinette, kitchen, and living room.

Other couples moved in that day and all the women brought things to eat. As we were getting acquainted, some of the others were consuming alcoholic beverages. One of the couples was a recently hired high school coach and his wife. They told us they had been lectured by the Orange City School Board about what they could and could not do. Drinking of any sort was frowned on. So, they were eating with us but not partaking in the alcohol.

Suddenly, there was a rap at the door. There stood the chief of police, all dressed up in his uniform.

"This is a raid," he said in an official voice.

The coach was about ready to jump out the window. He thought his job was gone. But it was just a joke.

Our first child, Linda, was born on January 12, 1952. We were happy to be living in the Kepp Apartments, as it was a much nicer place for us to be with a growing family.

MARY GETS WHEELS

Mary still didn't have a car. We had one child and another on the way. Every time we wanted to go anywhere, we had to empty my car of vet supplies.

Dr. Fisher's wife also did not have a car, and they had several children. One day, when I came in from answering some calls in the country, Dr. Fisher was in the office going over the books.

"You know, Neumann," Dr. Fisher said to me. "We have enough money here to do something."

"Like what?" I asked.

"We are going to buy two cars," he answered. "One for my wife and one for your wife."

We went to different dealers and bought two cars. When I took ours home to my wife, she was really happy!

There is an old saying, "Put a woman on wheels and there goes your meals." That didn't happen with Mary. She still got my meals, but she was tickled pink.

The girl who became my wife.

This white house was Mary's home in Ames.

The International pickup was still in use when Mary and I announced our engagement to my parents.

A shower of rice greeted Mary Virginia and me as we left First Methodist Church in Ames.

The registration to one of the first cars we owned.

Me and Mary in 1951.

CHAPTER TWELVE

A Home of Our Own

We lived at Kepp Apartments for three or four years. But when our son, David, was born in September 1955, we were living in a brand-new house we had built—a place with both a good story and a good lesson behind it.

THE WESTRA BOYS

We were open to renting, but we really wanted to buy or build a house. Mary was pregnant again, and our one-bedroom apartment was becoming too small. We had found a two-story house we liked; it obviously needed some fixing up, but we had saved some money.

I was eligible for a GI loan, so I went to the banker to talk about buying this particular house. To my surprise, he told me he could not give me a loan because I didn't have anything but my practice to stand as security. My interest in the practice was paid for, and I was eligible under the terms of the GI loan. *Period*. Yet they wouldn't do it.

One day, very shortly after that meeting, I was walking down the street from Woudstra's Meat Market and met a couple of men standing on the corner. One of the men was Mike Westra. The Westra brothers—Mike, John, and Henry—owned the junkyard near Northwestern College. They did a big business selling used parts for cars and machinery.

"Hey, Doc! I want to talk to you for a few minutes," called Mike. All the other men left so we could talk.

"I hear you are interested in buying a house," he continued.

I told him about the house and that the bank wouldn't lend me the money.

"Let's you and I look at it sometime," Mike said.

I arranged the time. Mike and I went through the house top to bottom. I pointed out what immediately needed fixing. But I also told him about our secondary plan: We either wanted to buy this house and fix it up or buy the empty lot on Concord Avenue. We had enough money for the lot, but we would need a loan to build a house on it.

Mike suggested we go look at the lot. He listened to me talk about our plan to build a basement to live in until we could build the upper story.

I almost fell over when Mike said he and his brothers would lend me the money to build, as much as we needed. This came as a real shock to me. Someone who didn't know much about me had enough faith to finance my home, basically no questions asked.

Mike said that when we decided how much money we needed, I should come over to his home to write the note. He lived with his brother, John. (Henry was the only Westra brother who was married.)

Some people in town disliked the Westra boys because they drank a lot. And I don't believe they were regular churchgoers. But here were three people—who I barely knew—who were going to lend me the money to build a home for my family.

Mary and I decided to go with our plan of building the basement on the lot and living in it until the upper story was complete.

I went to John Westra and told him how we were going to do it. We had figured out about how much money it would cost to build a basement and frame the house up. Then we could start working on the upper story as money became available.

John suggested we go to an attorney. At that meeting, I got another surprise.

"Mr. Westra, how do you want this note drawn up?" asked the attorney.

"Ask Dr. Neumann here," John replied. "He is the one who has to pay it off."

I was dumbfounded he would let me decide how to pay the note off.

As I needed money, the Westras just handed me the original note and told me to get it brought up to date. It was no small sum, as the total amount borrowed came to $30,000.

I never forgot how the Westra brothers trusted me, helping me through a difficult time in my life. These were men who were looked down on by a certain segment of the town's population. Yet when we needed help, they were the ones who gave it to us.

OUR HOME

David was born while we lived in our basement house. Penny, too. We were very comfortable there. In fact, Mary was in no big rush to get everything done. I was the one pushing to get aboveground.

"You don't want to be underground all the time," I would say to her. "Everyone wants to be up, aboveground, where you can look outside."

The framing was covered with black paperboard, which held it together. We put in storm windows where there were openings. Everything was weathertight.

That is how the house sat until we could afford to put the brick on it. Fred Vande Weerd did a beautiful job on the brickwork.

We continued to work on the inside as we had money to invest in it. Since plastering was my brother Darryl's business, he came to work on the inside walls. My mother wanted to help, so she came along. In 1963, we moved upstairs. Later, we insulated and finished the inside of the garage.

Mary did an excellent job designing our cabinets and choosing the wood. She was ahead of her time. Most kitchen cabinets built in Orange City in the 1950s had flat plywood surfaces. But Mary wanted the doors and drawers to have trim. Bernie Vander Aarde, the cabinetmaker, didn't want to put the trim on, though. They argued back and forth. Mary won, and soon everyone had to have trimmed cabinets.

Mary also designed the cupola on the garage that pipes in fresh air from the outside. She would have made a great interior designer. It's been over sixty years, and what she did still astonishes people.

We were able to finish and finance our house because we took our time. We worked as we had the funds, without borrowing a lot of money. The Westra boys helped us out, as did the Good Lord. Whenever we needed something, it always came...

Sometimes from unlikely places!

Me reading to my children Linda, David, and Penny Jo at our home.

Me and Mary at our home in Orange City.

Me at our kitchen table.

CHAPTER THIRTEEN

Mary, My Partner

My wife was a worker, not a complainer. When she didn't like something, she tried to rectify it. She didn't sit around.

OUR CHILDREN

Mary was always very proud of her family. She taught our children two real good rules:

1. *Nothing is free. You get what your work for.*
2. *Always save money for a rainy day.*

If I needed help, Mary—and later on, our children—always gave it to me.

For example, our son David would often help me at my practice. He had a solid understanding of veterinary medicine and would have made an excellent veterinarian. Instead, he chose to become a podiatrist (a career he excels in). As we drove from call to call, he would say, "Dad, you spend too much time in your truck on the road."

Our daughters also pursued medical careers. Linda, our oldest, went to college and trained to be a nurse. Later, she went back to school to become a nurse anesthetist. Penny Jo, the youngest of the three, is a surgical nurse. She programs robots to do surgical procedures.

Really, I can't say enough for Mary. Without her, I couldn't have had such a successful practice. Her stability at home, where she looked out for the interests of the children—plus the work she did in the practice—was a great help. Much is due to her working in the background.

TWO-WAY RADIOS

We used two-way radios during our early practice. Per the federal mandate, every time we talked on the radios we identified ourselves by saying, "This is KAB994." We also gave our car numbers. Dr. Fisher was car one; I was car two.

Base stations were kept in the office and in our homes. Mrs. Fisher and my wife would alternate weekends being home to answer the phone and direct us to farm calls. Using the two-way radios, we would report when we had finished a call. Then the wife on duty would tell us if and where there was more work to do. Because of this busy schedule, Mary didn't have the time to get out to all the activities she would have liked to participate in.

THE PHONE WOULD ALWAYS RING

I will say that as far as bringing up the kids, it was more Mary's job than mine. That's one thing I regret, but you couldn't do anything different. My practice with Dr. Fisher was growing, and it was always first for us—seven days a week, twenty-four hours a day. Veterinarians can't be clock-watchers—animals don't decide when they are going to be sick or in trouble.

This can put a strain on a family. I didn't get to see them as much as I wanted. I couldn't always go to the activities and events the children were involved in. It seemed as though every time I had a free moment, the phone would ring.

For example, one Christmas Eve we were to have a big party at our home. Mary's parents had come from Ames. But I ended up spending most of the night out in a barn, doing a cesarean on a cow that was in trouble. My father-in-law was with me when I got the call, so he spent his Christmas Eve in the barn, too. This all meant Mary didn't have the party she really wanted. But she didn't complain.

MARY IN THE BARN

Mary not only did the radios and bookkeeping for the practice, she helped out in surgery if we needed her, which often happened on Sundays or holidays.

I remember taking her along on a Sunday call once when she was pregnant. We had this cow—which was also pregnant—in the stanchion. The old cow was protesting quite vigorously. In order to get her under control, I had to put a bull lead in her nose. This would make it possible for us to pull the cow's head to the side to secure it.

I asked the farmer to hold the rope, but he refused to do it because he was afraid of the cow.

My wife stepped up and said, "Give me the rope. I will do it."

There was my pregnant wife, holding the rope of this pregnant cow. She thought nothing of it. The way she pitched in, it was sometimes hard to remember she was a city girl.

After the family was raised, Mary rode along with me to calls more often. She was always interested in how we practiced veterinary medicine.

TWO SHINERS

When we were busy with calls, we sometimes had to ask someone from the office to bring medicine out to a client. I would call Mary on the radio, requesting certain drugs and medicines, and give her directions to the client's farm.

One autumn day, she had to go to a farm northwest of Orange City. I told her to be careful on those intersections, because the tall corn blinded the corners.

I went about my business. Mary delivered the medicine, but not without a mishap. On her way home, she was traveling east on Highway 10. A westbound car made a left-hand turn in front of her. When they collided, Mary hit the steering wheel with the bridge of her nose.

When she came home, she told the kids (who were in junior high and high school), not to tell me she'd had an accident on a corner. Later, David told me he'd had a hard time controlling his laughter because she had two *very* noticeable black eyes.

"Did you deliver that medicine?" I asked Mary when I got home.

"Yes," she replied.

Then I asked, "What happened to you?"

She looked at me funny.

"You have two shiners," I told her.

The secret was out. She had to tell me about the accident.

MARY FAINTS

Because she had been answering the phone for so many years and heard us talking about cases, Mary was sometimes able to advise clients on what to do until a veterinarian arrived. Oftentimes, I would get to the case and find that the livestock owner was very appreciative because her advice had saved the patient's life.

Mary knew how to apply tourniquets, what to do for bloats, and what to do when a calf or foal delivery needed help. She knew many of the procedures that would alleviate pain or suffering in small animals.

The only time she failed me was one hot Sunday afternoon in the summertime. A client had dropped off a small lamb with a broken leg. He left, so I had no one to help me. I asked Mary to come to the office to assist in the procedure. It was very warm in the operating room, which might have played a part in what happened next.

Mary was holding the lamb's broken leg. I was just ready to set the pin when she fainted. In a flash, she gently slipped to the floor. I knew she hadn't hit her head, so I quickly finished pinning the lamb's leg before I went to her.

She was sheepish about that fainting incident. Every so often, she would bring up how she had just passed out that one summer.

A BROKEN LEG

By the 1990s I had cut my horse herd down to a couple saddle horses, a mule named Joe, and about six or eight Belgian draft mares.

Normally, I would hire a man to take care of them if I was gone. One time, I was called by the Amish in eastern Iowa to do some equine work. Hard as I tried, I couldn't find anyone who could feed my horses.

I was only going to be gone overnight. Our daughter, Linda, was home, so Mary said they could easily take care of the feeding. All they had to do was fill the hay feeders in the yard.

It was very cold weather, with temperatures down near zero. I gave instructions on how many bales to feed the horses in the morning and at night. At that time, we were feeding them small, rectangular bales that weighed 50 to 60 pounds.

I emphasized that the two of them were to go out *together* to do the job. But Mary was very independent, so in the morning, she went out there alone. She left the car on the road because there was too much snow on the farm yard. It was bitterly cold.

Mary went into the barn and up into the haymow. She opened the door and pushed out the required number of bales, then dragged each bale to the feeder. She cut the twine before tossing the loose hay into the feeder.

The feeder was a wooden box about 16 feet long and 8 feet wide—chest-high to the mares. It was mounted on skids. The snow piled in the yard meant there was a space about three or four inches in height between the bottom of the feeder and the ground. As Mary pulled a bale down to break it open and put it in the feeder, her right foot slid into the gap. She slipped as she turned to pick up the bale, shattering her right leg.

I had a black Labrador retriever at the time. The dog lived at the farm and stayed with her during the ordeal that followed.

The horses were milling around like they do at mealtime. They didn't harm Mary as she lay on the ground. She couldn't walk, so she dragged herself across the yard, to the fence by the shed where we had a telephone. The distance was…oh, I would say pretty close to sixty feet.

Mary climbed the fence with her broken leg by placing one knee between one of the slats and raising her other leg to get between the next slat. She had to climb up, get over the fence, and climb back down using this method.

Mary then made her way to the warm shed. She called home, where Linda was. Linda immediately went to the farm. Because of the deep snow, Mary crawled to the road and was waiting to be rescued by the time Linda arrived. Rather than going directly to the hospital, Mary insisted on stopping at home first to clean up. The Orange City medical doctors sent her to a hospital in Sioux City, where they operated on her leg.

Me and my lab, Blackie.

Meanwhile, I was doing horse work for the Amish clients. This was before cell phones, and the Amish do not have telephones. No one was able to contact me until the afternoon.

Once I was told of Mary's accident, I drove directly to the hospital in Sioux City. And I have to admit I was quite angry. I had *specifically* told them not to go out there alone.

Mary had fed livestock before, and she was very comfortable going alone, even though it was zero degrees outside with ice and snow on the ground.

The following morning, I went back to the hospital and met the doctor who had pinned and screwed her leg together. I asked him how bad the fractures were.

"You won't believe this, but there are fifty-two pieces of broken bone in there," he said. "If you don't believe me, count them."

He put the X-ray up on the viewer for me to see. Mary had done a very beautiful job of fracturing that leg into many pieces. To this day, I don't quite understand how she climbed that fence to get out of the yard and into the shed.

The moral of that story? There are some predicaments that can be avoided. That's the only time I really got angry with her. There should have been two people there. She might not have been able to get out of the yard. She could have been killed. Mary had grit, but it took a bit more than that for her to get out safely that wintry day.

A MARE FOALS

Another time when I was going to be gone, I asked Mary to keep an eye on a mare that was going to foal. I told her it would be good if she checked on her every few hours to see if she was having problems.

When I came home, I drove past the pasture and saw a young colt following its mother. I told Mary she had done a good job.

"You were fortunate," she said. "I never went to check."

MARY'S ANCESTRY

Mary Virginia had an interesting background, as far as her ancestry is concerned. Take, for example, the three Easterly brothers—George, Jacob, and Conrad—who came from the Palatinate region in Germany around 1700. (Mary's grandmother on her mother's side was an Easterly.)

George passed away shortly after his arrival in America. Jacob settled in Pennsylvania, with descendants moving into Ohio and Iowa. After Conrad married, he moved to Rockingham in the Shenandoah Valley of Virginia. They had two daughters and a son named George, who was born May 4, 1749.

Mary's ancesteral home in Tennesee.

The young George Easterly married Mary Harpine and moved his family to Greene County, Tennessee, in October 1796. They built their cabin home on the south side of the Nolichucky River.

They were frontier people during an interesting time in history. At the time of the Revolutionary War, there was quite a conflict between those backing the fight for independence and those against it. Neighbors were fighting neighbors. Barns were burnt and livestock stolen.

British troops were stationed in what is now the Carolinas. There, they would just help themselves to the available housing, food, livestock, and grain. When these frontiersmen were threatened by a British major, men from North Carolina, Tennessee, and Virginia rebelled.

Rather than waiting, these backwoodsmen voluntarily joined together as an armed force. They went over the mountains to the Carolinas to fight the British along a treeless ridge called Kings

Mountain. The frontiersmen's victory is often referred to as a turning point of the Revolutionary War. The British army was disheartened, while the colonists were greatly encouraged.

These men acquired the title "Over the Mountain Men." Some of them were Mary's ancestors.

Mary's grandmother, Etheline Eliza Easterly, married James Walter Scott. He was a relative of Winfield Scott, who also played a prominent role in America's history. In the war with Mexico, he was in charge of the American troops. Scott also served as Commanding General of the United States Army from 1841 to 1861, when he had to retire due to ill health.

We also believe that in Mary's Prather ancestry, there was a family in which nine sons were Methodist circuit-riding preachers. They had a prayer that has been passed down through the family:

"The Lord bless us and bind us, and tie our hands behind us, and throw us in the ditch, where the devil can't find us."

Mary was often called "Mary Virginia," simply because there were many other Marys in the close family. Her aunt, Mary Elizabeth, was her mother's youngest sister and just a few years older than Mary Virginia.

I often thought Mary inherited many good values from her ancestors, especially being thrifty, working hard, and sticking to her beliefs. If Mary believed in something, she believed in it; it was quite an accomplishment to get her to change her mind.

The thriftiness was helpful when the children needed or wanted something. She had money stashed away for all their needs. Clear up to their college years, she could always provide what they asked for. She saved everything and never threw anything away. That was her legacy, and she taught it to our children.

Mary never complained about the long hours I worked and was away from the family. She enjoyed the practice, her home, her house, and her flower gardens, which still bloom today. I often thought I was fortunate having Mary as a partner.

My wife, Mary Virginia.

CHAPTER FOURTEEN

Early Calls

When I started my career as a vet, I weighed 135 pounds and was quite agile. I was pretty green, but I got along fine. Still, a few of my earliest calls were nothing short of memorable.

OOPS!

One of my first calls was to John Vander Laan's farm on the northern edge of Orange City. I was to vaccinate forty small pigs for cholera. That was a small bunch, even for 1949.

The treatment at the time was a dose of serum and a dose of virus. Being the vaccinator required dexterity, since you had to hold a syringe in each hand. A bag of the cholera serum was attached to one of the syringes and hung around the vaccinator's neck.

First, the area under the pig's front legs was swabbed with disinfectant. The syringes were also dipped in disinfectant. The goal was to simultaneously give the pig subcutaneous doses of the serum and virus in its armpits.

I can still visualize John Vander Laan holding the pig up. Instead of hitting the armpit of the pig, I put the needle right through Mr. Vander Laan's hand. He didn't grimace or shout out in pain.

Instead, he said rather calmly, "We know we all have accidents once in a while."

OFFICE BOY

Another early call brought me to Jake P. Vander Zwaag's farm northeast of Orange City. When I drove onto the yard that day, it looked as though Mr. Vander Zwaag had prepared well. The neighbors were all there to help vaccinate the large number of pigs scheduled.

Whistling, I got out of my car and started to get my equipment ready.

"Who are you?" asked Mr. Vander Zwaag, in perhaps not the friendliest voice.

"I am the veterinarian," I answered.

"You look like the office boy," he retorted.

"Well, I am not," I replied. "I am the new vet."

"Just wait a minute," Mr. Vander Zwaag said before walking off to his house.

It was summer and the windows were open. We all could hear Mr. Vander Zwaag on the phone, talking to Dr. Fisher at the clinic.

"Just who did you send out? He looks like the office boy...Okay."

Mr. Vander Zwaag came back out and said, "Get your stuff ready, office boy. It's time to get vaccinating."

Whenever Mr. Vander Zwaag needed veterinary work done, he called the clinic and asked for that office boy.

YES, I CAN DO THAT

In vet school, students watched professors perform castrations on animals. But it wasn't until we were practicing that we actually did the operation ourselves.

One day, I was called to the Vander Wilt farm near Middleburg to treat a sick steer. When the farmer saw the castrating harness in the back seat of my car, he asked if I had time to castrate a horse. I was scared stiff, but I said, "Yes, I can do that."

The farmer brought out a great, big, five-year-old Percheron. He called the neighbors to help hold down the horse. I swallowed hard and set my mind to doing the job.

I got the job done well, and when I jerked the casting harness off the horse I was no longer afraid of the task.

TONSILS...ARE YOU SURE?

One day, I was called to the De Haan farm north of Orange City to castrate a horse. Before the sixties, the procedure was usually performed with just the farmer and veterinarian present. The children were sent to the house, while the women just automatically disappeared.

Mr. De Haan took Dr. Fisher and me down a grassy lane to a tree in the pasture. His two young sons accompanied the procession. They climbed the tree to have a bird's-eye view.

The men got busy.

"What are you doing, Doc?" asked one of the boys.

"Taking out his tonsils," answered Dr. Fisher.

A few minutes later, one of the boys had this to say:

"I have had my tonsils out…but they didn't come from down there."

A BROKEN NECK

It was July, and Dr. Fisher was gone to the lakes in Minnesota to fish and relax. I got a call to go to Milt Bogaard's farm northwest of town to check a cow. Jerry Te Paske accompanied me. He was a local boy who was interested in veterinary medicine. He regularly rode along on calls through his high school years and when he was home from college. He later became a veterinarian and owned several clinics in Washington, D.C., before retiring to a farm in Maryland where he raises stock cows.

Mr. Bogaard had the cow in a stanchion in the barn. I examined the cow to try to determine why she couldn't become pregnant. This was a wild cow, prone to kicking. I soon ascertained that all the nice, big Holstein needed was a dose of hormone. When I stepped over the gutter to get the dose of medicine and syringe, I noticed it was full of manure and cow urine.

I asked Mr. Bogaard to hold the cow's tail up over her back, which would help keep her from kicking. The idea was to give the cow a shot in the muscle at the top of her rump. As I was stepping across the gutter, the cow kicked me in the knees, tossing me up in the air. When I landed, my head hit the gutter's edge and knocked me out.

The cow continued her attack, practically kicking my left ear off. Mr. Bogaard and Jerry Te Paske pulled me through the manure to safety.

When I came to, Mr. Bogaard was fanning me and asking if I was okay. The men moved me to a cleaner spot. I realized my neck was broken, and I ordered the fellows to let me lie still. They brought an ironing board from the house and very gently slid me onto it, carried me up to the farmhouse, and put me in the screened-in porch.

Since Orange City still did not have an ambulance, I again took a ride in the Van Etten hearse to the Doornink Hospital. That hearse required plenty of cleaning later, since I was covered with manure. The smell stayed even after my clothes had been exchanged for a hospital gown. The nurses and doctor held their noses and wore masks when caring for me.

My neck was broken in two places. That same Van Etten hearse transferred me to St. Luke's, a larger hospital in Sioux City. There I was X-rayed again before they put me in bed in traction, where I stayed for three or four weeks. They were expecting me to stay longer, but I healed quickly.

The orthopedic surgeon was an elderly gentleman who talked pretty rough. When I was to ready to leave the hospital, he wanted to put a neck brace on me. I told him no, I could not operate that way. Plus, I was afraid I would have to wear the brace for years.

The surgeon cussed at me and told me he didn't want to see me in a week. He had quite a mastery of the English language. I was very careful with my neck. I didn't want to see him in a week…or any other time for that matter.

CHAPTER FIFTEEN

Some Extra-Memorable Calls

Part I

I never knew what to expect when I got into my car to respond to a call. Even the most routine call could become interesting.

But there are a few extra-memorable incidents that really stick out in my mind.

WILD COWS

One time, a client purchased fourteen western cows. He called the clinic to have someone come out and dehorn them.

They were a wild bunch. The farmer had unloaded them from the truck into a tin cattle shed, which was pretty much escape-proof since it was very tightly boarded. That was a good idea, since the cattle were looking for a way to escape.

The farmer had lined up plenty of help for the job, but it wasn't safe for anyone to enter the cattle shed. We decided to remove a tin panel from the roof and gently herd the cows from above while others banged on the shed to sort them off one by one into the chute.

The last cow that came into the chute had a really nice sweep to her horns. But she went through so fast it was impossible for the chute man to get the head gate closed. The wild cow was now on the loose, and those horns looked even more menacing out in the open than they did when she was in captivity.

The chute operator climbed the chute, but I was out in the open. That cow was looking to get me. I jumped the fence, but the cow—in close pursuit—easily sailed over right behind me.

The door was open on a machine shed, so I ran inside and jumped up to hold onto a rafter. The cow followed me. With her horns, she caught the belt loop of my jeans, tearing them off and leaving me in my long underwear.

The men came inside, not sure what condition they would find me in. When they saw me dangling from the rafters in my underwear, they stood around laughing their heads off.

"You get rid of that *** cow and get me down," I shouted.

A FIST FIGHT

Another memorable farm visit happened one snowy evening near Maurice. Because the roads were bad, the vet clinic closed early for the day. Just as we were locking the doors, a call came in.

A woman said she had a sow that could not deliver her pigs. I told Dr. Fisher I would take the call. My hands were small, which worked better for pulling pigs.

Dr. Fisher, said, "Well, the roads aren't that good. Why don't I just ride along in case you need an extra hand shoveling?"

So he did.

We got to the farm and found the client's son feeding the steers. He took us into the barn where the sow was bedded down in straw, trying to deliver her pigs. Dr. Fisher restrained the sow, holding her front leg up. This prevented the sow from getting up. I began delivering the pigs.

After a time, the farmer came into the barn. He had a reputation for going to town in the afternoon and coming home drunk…which was exactly the condition he was in that night.

The farmer immediately began insulting Dr. Fisher. He took it for a while. But as the man continued his abusive language, Dr. Fisher dropped the leg of the sow and stood up, demanding the farmer take back what he had said.

"No, I will not," said the man, taking a swing at Dr. Fisher.

Dr. Fisher whacked him one, and the man fell to the ground. But the farmer got up, swinging his fist again. This happened three times, and each time he fell to the ground.

I finished my work with the sow and heard these surprising words:

"The missus sent me out here to invite you to supper," said the farmer. "You will stay, won't you?"

We agreed and went in for supper. Dr. Fisher and I had a friendly conversation with the family and an enjoyable evening at the table.

BUMBLEBEES

At one time, bumblebees were a terror to men and boys raking hay, especially around red clover. Hay raking was often accomplished with horses, and if the horses came upon a nest of bumblebees they would spook or try to run away. Sometimes the results were disastrous. This wasn't just a problem in the fields; a bumblebee nest in a barn could also cause problems.

I was called to a farm to treat six stock cows suffering from foot rot. As was normal in my early days of practice, the farmer did not own a chute or have a working pen.

The old, rundown barn was divided into two sections. The cows were grouped in one section. Once again, they were wild. The plan was to rope a cow, bring it into the other section, and have my assistant pull the rope through the hole in the manger to secure it. I would then treat the cow and turn her out.

The first cow was easily caught. When they pulled up the rope, she bumped into the wooden manger...and out rolled bumblebees from a hidden nest. They were not happy to be disturbed, and they let us know it.

The cow was bellowing from being stung by the bees. The farmer and I were up on the wall trying to stay away from both bees and cows. Because the other five cows were also being attacked by the bees, they broke into the pen where we were. The whole outfit tore around in the pen until they smashed through the door and bolted outside.

My assistant was hanging on another side wall in an attempt to stay out of the way. When we got to him, he was already going into shock. He had been stung multiple times. The farmer rushed him to the hospital in Le Mars, where he recovered.

The cows had all fled, so the job was rescheduled for another day.

JUST WHAT DID YOU SEE?

One Sunday morning, a client called. He had a really sick steer. It wouldn't be long until they left for church, but if I came out right away he would be able to help me. I told him I would be right over.

I found the farmer in the barn, where he was finishing putting the steer in the chute. We needed hot water, so he told me to go to the house and get some from the kitchen sink. So that is where I went.

There was the missus, without a stitch of clothing on, by the kitchen sink. She heard the door open and turned around. When she saw it was me and not her husband, she let out a yelp. With one mighty leap, she cleared the kitchen table, escaping into another room. Despite my shock, I managed to get the water before going back out to the barn to care for the sick steer.

I told her husband what had happened.

"I have told her over and over again not to walk around the house naked," her husband said. "I warned her she was going to get caught someday."

A few weeks later, I was back to that farm, doing some more work. The neighbors were also there. Once the work was done, we were all invited into the house for afternoon lunch. I was embarrassed to go in, but there was no way I could avoid it.

The lady of the farm was going around the table, filling each man's cup with coffee.

"Now, Doc," she said when she was pouring my coffee. "What exactly did you see the other day?"

"Not a thing," I replied. "Not a thing."

With those words, she relaxed and felt much better, I am sure.

DON'T GO IN FOR COFFEE

Dr. Fisher had warned me never to accept this one client's invitation for coffee. Whenever I was asked in, I always managed to use the excuse that I had another call or was expected somewhere else.

But one morning, I had a very early call to this farm. When I got there, both the mister and missus were outdoors. They were an elderly couple who kept a little livestock on their farm—pigs, dairy cows, cattle, and chickens.

On previous visits, I had noticed their chore clothes were never very clean. But that happens sometimes, or so I thought. This time when I was asked in, there was no way to politely decline. So, I went in for coffee.

The floor looked like it had never been swept. Clutter and filth everywhere. I sat down by the table.

The farmwife put her apron on. She took a cup out of the warming compartment above the wood stove and wiped the inside with her apron. I started to feel a little queasy. Then, she used a ladle to fill my cup with coffee from the reservoir of the stove.

"We had fried chicken for supper last night," she said as she handed me the cup. "I could easily warm some up for you."

I had noticed the pan of chicken on the stovetop. I politely declined but thanked her for the coffee and went on my way. They were good-hearted people, just used to living that way. I never went back in their house again, despite their many invitations.

ONE SOURCE OF HOT WATER

Not only did cars serve as transportation for veterinarians, they stored our tools of the trade. It was definitely better than the horse and buggy Dr. Roach used before he changed to a Model A. The main thing we lacked, though, was warm water to use in our work and clean up after a call.

One night, I was called to George Baker's farm. It was the middle of winter, and there was plenty of snow on the ground. Like normal, I took my bucket to the barn and told Mr. Baker I needed warm water. He thought for a moment before answering that he would fill the bucket.

It didn't take very long, and soon Mr. Baker was back with a bucket of really nice warm water. When the work was done, I remembered to thank him for it.

"George, now that was a really nice bucket of warm water."

"Oh, that's right. I got to remember to fill my tractor with water again," he said.

Rather than purchasing antifreeze, some farmers would run their tractors continuously to keep the water in the radiator from freezing. They would drain the radiators when they were finished using their tractors for the day.

It wasn't until 1959, after a car accident, that I purchased a Ford pickup truck with a box designed for veterinary use. There were compartments for hot and cold water, plus a small refrigerator. Now, that was something!

TREATING RINGWORM

One day, I received a call from the nurse at Northwestern College. There was a ringworm problem in a girls' dormitory. The medication prescribed by a local doctor was not clearing up the fungal infection. She knew we treated livestock for ringworm and wondered whether we ever got infected.

"We sure do," I answered.

"How do you treat it?" she asked.

"Well, we just use what we give the livestock," I said.

"Can I get some of that medication?" she asked.

"Yes, you can if you are going to use it on livestock."

"Okay," she said.

Later, she picked up the medicated cream.

That was the last I heard of it for a while. Then, the phone rang one day. One of the local doctors was on the line. He was highly agitated that I had given the medicine to the college nurse.

One of the girls was a patient in his office. He had asked her how the ringworm was doing when she came in for an appointment.

"It's all gone," she said.

"So the last medication I gave you cleared it up," the doctor answered.

"No, we got some medication from a veterinarian," she explained.

The doctor threatened to sue me, as it wasn't legal for me to treat humans. I told him he would look pretty silly explaining to the court that because he couldn't cure the ringworm, they'd had to go to a veterinarian.

Down went the telephone. Needless to say, our relationship was strained for many years.

PENNY JO'S SWOLLEN ANKLE

One time, my daughter was injured at a basketball tournament in Orange City. An X-ray determined that her ankle was not fractured, only badly sprained with a large amount of swelling.

She wanted to keep playing basketball, but her ankle hurt too much.

"I have some liniment we could apply," I offered.

"No. I am *not* taking any horse medicine," she insisted. This went on for days. She was in a turmoil, as the day of her next game kept getting closer. Finally, she asked for the liniment.

I told her it needed to be applied three times a day. In a few days, the swelling went down and she was able to play.

Her coach asked me about the liniment. I told him, "It works… but it's not licensed for humans."

CHAPTER SIXTEEN

Some Extra-Memorable Calls

Part II

Many of my clients became my friends. I enjoyed getting to know them and sharing the adventures of farm life with them. But there were a few instances that were definitely *not* covered in my college textbooks.

FARM BURGLARIES

Sometimes, when we arrived at a call, the farmer was not home. Many times, the farmer's house and buildings were unlocked. They left notes, telling us to use whatever we needed. If it was necessary for us to go in the house for water, we could do that. I *always* stressed to my men not to take anything. If they did, they would be done working for me.

Occasionally, property and livestock were stolen from farms. Gasoline was a popular item for stealing, since tanks were often unlocked. But for the most part, the rural areas were relatively free of thievery. Myself, I had just a few run-ins with farm burglars.

The first story requires some background information. For a time, Saturday night was the big shopping night in Orange City. Farmers brought their eggs to town, where there were buyers for their produce.

The women shopped and purchased groceries while their husbands visited and did business. But at some point over the years, the big shopping night changed from Saturday to Thursday evening.

Our office was open on Thursdays. Clients would come in just to visit or schedule work for the following week.

On to the story. It was late fall, and much of the corn had been harvested. As was the custom in those days, Joe Kleinhesselink had turned his cows out into a harvested field. (This was the Joe Kleinhesselink near Boyden; there were three Joe Kleinhesselinks farming in the area.)

He called me and said he and his family were going to town for Thursday shopping, but he had a sick cow in the barn he wanted me to look at. He thought the cow had eaten too much corn.

The farm had a long driveway off a gravel road. It was dark when I drove on the yard, but a light helped me see a bit. I noticed a stock truck parked next to the hog house door. I could hear pigs squealing.

I just figured someone must be loading pigs. That wouldn't have been uncommon, since loads of livestock were often brought to the Sioux City or Sioux Falls stock yards on Thursdays for the Friday sales. So I didn't think too much of it.

After treating the cow and turning her out, I went back to my truck. When I glanced at the stock truck, I could just see the outline of two men in the dim light. I never saw the third man, but I could hear him down by the truck.

"Hey Doc, need any help?" hollered one of the men in a friendly voice.

"No, I am done," I answered. "Thank you."

Waving good-bye, I left the farm.

The next morning, I got a telephone call from Sheriff Harry Dykstra. "Were you up to Joe Kleinhesselink's farm near Boyden last night?" he asked.

"Yes."

"Did you see anyone?"

"Not really, but there was someone loading hogs."

"Can you come up to my office and talk to me?" he asked. "On second thought, stay in your office. I will come right over."

A very short time later, Sheriff Dykstra arrived at my office.

"A load of hogs was stolen from Joe Kleinhesselink's farm last night. There have been lots of hogs stolen in Plymouth and Sioux Counties lately," he explained. "We have been keeping it quiet, but so far no one has seen any trace of the thieves."

I was really surprised, as I had talked to one of them and was aware that there were three men in the crew. They had stayed far away from me and out of the light, so I was unable to give any description of them.

When I asked what would have happened if I had walked down there, the sheriff said I probably would have had a tire iron wrapped around my head.

The men were never caught, but the stealing stopped all of a sudden.

Another time, the robbers were not so fortunate...and yet, in a way, they were.

It was church time one Sunday night. I was called to a farm east of town. My route took me past Henry Huitink's farm—Henry of Gerrit, not to confuse anyone with the other Henry Huitink in the area. I knew him and his farm's set-up pretty well, since my pasture land adjoined with his.

It was summertime, and as I came around the curve I saw a station wagon sitting in the road with its back door open. I realized someone was putting something into the back of the car. When the man saw me, he slammed the door shut. In a hurry, he got in his car and took off down the road, leaving a cloud of dust. At the same time, I noticed someone step backward into the cornfield.

I thought this was strange, since almost every farmer would have been in church at that time of night.

Henry Huitink's farm also had a long driveway. If someone were to steal something from his farm, they would easily be caught red-handed because a person could be in the driveway before the thief had a chance to get away.

I stopped my truck to call my wife on the two-way radio and requested that she call the sheriff, as I thought a burglary was happening at the Henry Huitink farm.

My truck windows were open, and my conversation was overheard by two big, strong young men who had been hiding in the cornfield. They came out into the open and guessed I was a veterinarian based on the appearance of my truck.

"Doc, you didn't need to call the sheriff. We were just helping ourselves to some sweet corn," one of them explained.

"Ah-hum," I said. "We will just wait for the sheriff."

The men started walking down the ditch toward me. I reached behind my seat for my gun. Once I had it out, I told the men to sit down with their hands behind their heads.

One did. The other kept walking toward me. He started to come up the road bank.

"I'm no match for you physically," I said. "But I will shoot you if you threaten me." I cocked the gun and pointed it toward him.

Fortunately, he backed off and sat down by the other man. The sheriff soon arrived on the scene. It turns out they had been robbing the house, transporting the items through the cornfield to the station wagon. The men were recently returned soldiers from the Viet Nam War and were looking to furnish their rented house.

The sheriff took the two men into custody. The third man was also apprehended. The sheriff went to get Henry Huitink from church.

Mr. Huitink had been captured by the German army during World War II. While he was being transported to a prison camp, he and another man had escaped from the moving train. Both men were picked up by the French underground. He had then fought with the French freedom fighters. He felt sorry for these three veterans and chose not to prosecute them.

I told the sheriff those men could have easily overpowered me, and I wondered what would have happened if I had shot one of them. He soberly told me I would have been in a lot of trouble. He said if I ever saw anything suspicious again, the best thing to do would be to call the sheriff's office.

A HANGING INTERRUPTED

It was mid-morning when I finally got around to answering a call that had come in earlier that day about treating a cow. I found the cow in the stanchion, with no sign of the farmer. That wasn't unusual. As I was beginning my assessment of the cow, I glanced around the empty barn.

I noticed a pair of boots where the ladder met the haymow. They were pointed out, away from the ladder. Obviously, that meant I wasn't alone in the barn, so I went to investigate.

What I saw sent shivers down my spine. The farmer was standing there with his back to the ladder and a noose around his neck. He was getting ready to jump.

An education at vet school does not train you for situations like this. Yet, I instinctively knew I had to do something. So I started talking to the farmer, calling him by name.

"What are you going to do, hang yourself?" I asked. "I can't let you take your life. Let's take that rope off your neck. I have a pocket knife that could do it, but I would hate to cut that good rope. How about if I take it off?"

He never said anything, leaving me to do all the talking. He just stood there on the ladder.

As I started to climb the ladder to take the noose off, the farmer began to cry. Any time a full-grown man begins to cry, there is something majorly wrong. I helped him down the ladder to the barn floor, talking to him all the time.

Through bits and pieces, I was able to discern that there were serious problems in his marriage.

The farmer's wife was home. She was shocked to see us, especially to see her husband in tears. I told her what had been happening in the barn. She didn't know what to do; she was very upset.

I suggested that she call their minister to come over. I said I would wait until he showed up. She made a pot of coffee, and we waited in the kitchen for the minister to come. When he did, I left.

I was called back to the farm many times after this incident. Years later, after the couple retired and moved to town, we would occasionally bump into each other. I never did hear another word about what happened in the barn. They must have gotten things worked out.

SAVING A LIFE FROM A CORN PICKER

Once, a call came in that a herd of sick pigs required a veterinarian's care. It was fall, so farmers were going full speed at the harvest. When I drove onto the yard, the lady of the house came out and instructed me to go to the cornfield where her husband was picking corn.

When I got there, the farmer was pulling his mangled hand out of the corn picker. After the tractor was shut off, I took a tourniquet out of my truck and applied it to the farmer's lower arm. Once the injured hand was wrapped in clean towels, we got in my truck. The farmer was in a bit of shock.

We stopped at the farm house to let his wife know about the accident and that we were on our way to the hospital. She followed in her own vehicle.

Corn pickers were notoriously hard on farmers' hands. This farmer lost fingers and a part of his hand in the accident. Later, I went back to care for the pigs.

A CRYING WOMAN

Upon entering the office after answering calls in the country, Ed Reinders, my regular office man, met me and said, "You have a big problem in your back office. A woman is in there, crying. She is waiting for you."

With plenty of misgivings, I walked back to the office to find out what was going on. There is nothing worse than a lady crying. And she was, indeed, *crying*.

Once she calmed down, she told me the story.

"I have a grandson, who is old enough to crawl," she said. "My husband feeds the dog on the porch. We weren't paying close attention to my grandson. He crawled to where the dog was eating, and the dog bit him in the face quite severely."

She told me the kids would not come over again until the dog was gone. Her husband said the dog was his and that it wasn't the dog's fault. The boy shouldn't have been near the dog when it was eating. He refused to get rid of it.

"I own half of everything on the farm," she exclaimed. "I want *my* half of the dog killed!"

It was at this point I said to myself, *Neumann, this isn't your problem. Just go home and go to bed. When you get up in the morning, maybe everything will be different.*

But circumstances dictated that I had to handle the problem while she was in the office.

"Can't you work things out with your husband?" I asked. We argued back and forth.

Finally, it was decided that I would put down "her half of the dog." Then I would leave the dog there for her husband to bury. She would explain to him how it had happened.

The plan was to be executed on Saturday night, when they came to town to shop and visit. She was to call me from the grocery store when they arrived.

I contacted Al Schuller, a local farmer and one of my regular helpers, and told him about the job. He was to meet me at the farm as soon as I called him.

When we got to the farm, we found a very mean dog. He was chained to the garage, which was in plain view of anyone travelling on the gravel road going past the farm. Of course, at this time Saturday night was still the night most farm families came to town to do their weekly shopping and visiting. As the families went by, they recognized our vehicles and tooted their horns in recognition.

We tried to catch the dog, but I finally realized it was an impossible task. He was really mean, and he meant it. Time was passing, and we had to get the job done before the family came home. So, I gave up trying to catch the dog to give him an injection and instead shot him in the head with a .22 rifle.

The dog died instantly, but to complicate matters it bled all over the lawn and sidewalk, staining everything a beautiful, deep red.

Now what?

We looked for some buckets and scrub brushes to clean up the premises. All this had to be done in haste, because we didn't want to be caught in the act. We made it out of there safely and left the dog behind as planned.

The next morning, I went to the office bright and early, as I always did. There was the lady, sitting in her car and crying. Her husband was so angry when he saw the dead dog that she didn't tell him what had happened, like she had promised.

"He is going to find out who shot his dog," she said. "He is going to give that person the same treatment they gave the dog."

She told me her husband had to finish milking before he went to ask the neighbors if they knew who had been at their farm while they were gone to town the night before. He had his shotgun ready.

I knew it wouldn't take him long to learn I had done the shooting. The neighbors had seen us there when they were on their way to town. I thought there was a good possibility he would carry out his plan.

After she left, I went immediately to the sheriff's office. When I told Sheriff Harry Dykstra, who was my friend, he laughed.

"I can't do anything, Doc," he said. "Not until he commits a crime. At this point, he hasn't."

This didn't make me feel very good. I did some thinking. I knew what church the farmer and his wife went to, so I went to their pastor's home. While the pastor finished his breakfast, I told him my whole story, emphasizing that it would not take long for the farmer to realize it was me who had taken care of the dog…and that the man was carrying a loaded shotgun.

"I think I better go out there right away," said the pastor.

He did, and I never heard anything more about the incident. We continued to do veterinary work for the family for years, until they retired. The dog was never discussed, not even once.

I learned one lesson with this escapade: You are in big trouble when confronted with a weeping woman, especially when she wants you to put down her half of a dog.

A RING AND A CHAIN

I was dehorning calves, and a yearling bull was in the herd. The farmer was planning to save him to be a herd bull.

Do you want him to have a ring and chain in his nose?" I asked.

The ring and chain were a safety measure. If attacked, the farmer could grab the chain and turn the bull's head.

"Yes, but it will take me a bit of time to find some chain," he answered.

"We'll wait," I assured him. "The bull is in the chute, so he's not going anywhere."

In a short while, the farmer was back with a two-foot length of chain. The bull ring and chain were put in. It was all in a day's work, but I didn't realize how important our desire to do a thorough job was until later.

As the bull matured, he turned mean. One day, he attacked the farmer and got him in a corner. The farmer only escaped by grasping the chain and pushing the bull's head away.

SWEET CLOVER

Dr. Fisher was gone on vacation. It was Sunday morning, and I was dressed in my suit to go to church. Mary and I were ready to put the kids in the station wagon when we heard the telephone ring.

It was a client over by Sioux Center who I had worked with for years. He was highly excited, talking quickly in his half-Dutch, half-English accent.

His cattle had gotten into the sweet clover. They were bloating right in front of his eyes. Some had already died.

I told him to get a butcher knife and begin stabbing them in the rumen to let the gasses escape. I would be out there as quickly as I could.

"Come out right away, right away," he begged.

I left Mary with the kids. She stayed home to answer the phone. I went right out to the farm to take care of the cattle.

I was still in my Sunday suit. I spent the rest of the morning working to save the cattle. We had to open up each animal's rumen to let the gases escape, then stitch the tissues back together.

After that day, the farmer never did any more business with me. I wondered about it until I ran into him on the street one day.

"Doc Neumann, I always wanted to talk to you," he said. "I have nothing against you. You always did good work for me. But Dr. Vermeer goes to my church and I feel I should have him do my veterinary work."

"You do as you please," I answered kindly.

He walked away, and I thought of my wife, who had stayed home to answer the phones—not only that Sunday but on many other days. I also couldn't help but think of all those cows I saved in my "go-to-meeting" clothes. They were ruined, and my shoes were a mess.

But that was my job.

AN ANSWER TO A PRAYER

A call came in one day that a cow needed treatment. It was routine. As with many calls, the cow would be in the stanchion. The farmer would leave a note, telling me what I was to do with the cow when I was done treating it. Likewise, I would leave a note with my diagnosis and detailed instructions if the farmer needed to perform more treatments.

When I drove on the yard, a stock truck with a rack was backed up to the southwest door of the barn. I heard a terrific racket, including a person yelling.

What's this about? I thought.

When I opened the door on the south side of the barn, I saw a huge Holstein bull in the west pen. The bull had been borrowed by a farmer to service some cows. He and the truck driver were returning the bull to the owner.

When the truck driver opened the end gate on the truck, the bull came charging out. It chased the truck driver down the chute into the barn. The bull was very angry. In one corner lay the truck driver. The bull was trying to kill him by smashing him with its head. The only reason the truck driver was still alive was because he was able to grab the chain in the bull's nose and push its head to the side.

I grabbed a nearby pitchfork and climbed over the fence into the pen. I managed to distract the bull long enough for the truck driver to escape.

Once we were both on the other side of the fence, he thanked me and said he had been losing his strength. It wouldn't have been long until he wasn't able to keep the bull's head away.

"It sure is a good thing I came along, since you are here all alone," I said.

"I wasn't alone," he answered. "When we unloaded the bull, the farmer was with me. When I let the bull out of the truck, I couldn't get away fast enough. The farmer escaped. I don't know where he is."

I heard a little noise in the truck cab. When I opened the door, there was the farmer on his knees, praying for help.

"It worked," I said, smiling. "Your prayers were answered."

CHAPTER SEVENTEEN

A Few Trips to the Emergency Room

Each morning when I left for work, there was no guarantee I would return that night in the same physical condition I had left in. Working conditions were not always ideal, and accidents can and did happen. Sometimes all I needed was a quick trip to the emergency room; other times I needed a hospital stay.

STITCHES NEEDED

There was a cholera outbreak among pigs in the Orange City area one July, when it was very hot and humid. A client decided to be proactive and called me in to vaccinate his sow herd when he learned a neighbor's pigs had cholera.

Normally, this type of job was scheduled for early morning, before the heat of the day. But this time, that wasn't possible. So we started right after dinner, about one o'clock.

The sows were big. Two or three at a time were maneuvered into a small pen. I would sit on the sows while I vaccinated behind their ears with the serum and virus. At the same time, one of the farmer's neighbors was hosing the sows down to prevent them from overheating. Because they had a habit of lying down, the sows were already covered with manure. Now they were also sopping wet.

So was I, with water, manure, human sweat—you name it.

We finished around five o'clock. On the way home, I stopped to castrate a stallion, an appointment that had been scheduled for after the sow vaccination. The owner of the stallion had also been helping with the sows, so we had both just left the first farm to travel to his farm.

When I went down with the castrating knife, the horse jerked his leg a little bit, causing me to cut quite a chunk out between my thumb and first finger. But I finished the job, including stitching the horse.

After bandaging my hand, I alerted my wife to call the hospital so they would be ready for me...or so they thought. My assistant, Al Schuller, stayed with me. And so two very smelly, very dirty men entered the clean, sterile emergency room at Grossman Bushmer Hospital.

The emergency room nurse pinched her nostrils shut with her fingers.

"Oh, just take your fingers off, inhale two or three times, and then you will have it all," I suggested with a smile.

The doctor and his wife had just gotten ready to leave the house and go out for supper when the call came. It was a routine emergency that they didn't expect to take too long, so she came along. They would go on with their plans after he was finished with me.

The doctor arrived and stitched me up. Before he left, he ordered the nurses to disinfect the room from top to bottom and get maintenance to do a thorough cleansing.

His wife, who had been sitting in the waiting room with my assistant, told her husband she was no longer hungry and just wanted to go home.

DIAGNOSIS: RUPTURED LIVER

One day in late fall, I was called to deworm four horses southeast of Akron. At that time, the dewormer was not in liquid form. It was a pill that had to be administered orally with a balling gun. It was a normal procedure that I had plenty of experience with.

The four horses were in a relatively small outdoor pen on the north side of the barn. The ground was frozen, but there wasn't any snow cover. The owner said his horses were nervous…in other words, the farmer was too afraid to do the job himself.

Peter Bonthuis was my assistant that day. He was not only an excellent horseman, but also a very good man in general and a great helper. I caught one of the spooked horses and put a twitch on him. (A twitch is an instrument that, if applied properly, will sedate a horse.)

The owner was holding the horse in the middle of the yard. Mr. Bonthuis was handling the twitch. I stepped up to the right side of the horse and administered one pill, watching the horse all the time.

Horses are *gazers*. There are only two times a horse will look a person in the eye. One is when they are going to die. The other is when they intend to do you bodily harm. A good thing to remember is that a horse's hind leg will scare you, but the front legs will kill you.

When I saw the horse looking directly at me, I warned the farmer and Mr. Bonthuis to be careful. This horse was going to throw a fit.

Quick as lightning, the horse reared up when I attempted to administer a second pill. He struck me in the stomach area with his right hoof, right under the ribs. That kick sent me sailing through the air. My flight was stopped when I hit the barn, about five feet above the ground. The four horses ran around the small pen, stepping on me as I laid next to the barn.

An ambulance transported me to the Orange City hospital, where Dr. Grossman examined me. He diagnosed a possible ruptured liver.

I had to lay very still on my back for a week, while they constantly monitored my blood pressure and gave me plenty of medicine. If the bleeding hadn't stopped, they would have had to do surgery. Thankfully, it healed without a procedure.

Needless to say, I did not go back to those horses. I doubt very much they were ever dewormed.

AN ACCIDENTAL VACCINATION

Repeating syringes haven't always been available, which sometimes made administering vaccines a challenge. A syringe would hold 20 ccs, but a dosage of red nose (or infectious bovine rhinotracheitis) vaccine was 2 ccs. To make sure we administered a proper dose, a wing nut was set at the correct amount.

One day, a farmer north of Hospers called about his black Angus stock cows needing to be vaccinated for red nose and bovine virus diarrhea.

These stock cows were a bit on the nervous side. Inside the barn, we used the wall and two steel gates to make an alley that held four cows. The cows were vaccinated before being set free to go outside. The next four cows were then sorted off and moved into the alley.

I had just filled a syringe and was walking toward the makeshift alley. I hadn't even gotten the wing nut set. The next group of cows pushed against the gates. The chain broke loose, causing a gate to swing toward me. I put my arms out to protect myself, but the gate hit me with so much force that it drove me backward. As the gate hit me, I felt something in my abdominal area.

The syringe fastened to the 1-inch, 14-gauge needle emptied its entire contents into my peritoneal cavity. It was cold, and I could feel the vaccine burn as it moved down between my intestines.

As quick as I could, I got out to my car to get some epinephrine into a small needle and syringe. I sat on a bale and told the farmer that if I started to act goofy or passed out, he had to inject that syringe right into a muscle in my arm. He wanted to call the doctor's office, but I told him not to leave me alone. I would need the shot immediately if I started to pass out. When no side effects developed, we went right back to work.

Once the job was finished, I went to the hospital. Dr. Grossman was looking at the puncture wound when another doctor came in. He had some questions for me.

"Was the needle sterile?"

"Sure, I had just done forty head of cows," I answered.

"Are you sure it went in the peritoneal cavity?"

The questions seemed so foolish to me.

For hours, my blood pressure was monitored every fifteen minutes. My blood count went way up. I was given antibiotics and orders not to go back to work.

But I did go back.

The one thing I *never* did again was walk around with a filled syringe with the needle on the end.

ALONG FOR THE RIDE

It was a typical Iowa December. Cold, frozen ground, but no snow yet. Christmas was just a few weeks away. A call came in to treat a steer with hoof rot on a farm near Hawarden.

The farmer said the steer was in a pen in the barn. The minute we opened the top half of the wooden door to the pen, the steer vaulted over the bottom half. It took off running through the grove, joining the rest of the cattle in the oat stubble. ("Stubble" is the term for a field that has been harvested, but the plant stalks have been left standing for animals to graze on and prevent erosion.)

"We will never get that steer back," said the farmer.

"Sure, we can," I reassured him. "All it needs is one shot of penicillin. I'll get my rope, and we'll catch him that way."

So we got in the farmer's car and drove alongside the grazing steer. I was in the passenger seat and had my door open. I was sitting sideways with my feet on the car's edge, concentrating on making my lariat ready to throw. I didn't notice the steer had taken off running around the front of the car. He was now on the driver's side.

The farmer put the car in reverse and stepped on the gas to get closer to the steer. I fell out and landed right behind the right-side front wheel. The farmer didn't notice, since he was paying close attention to the steer. As the car was about to drive over me, I grabbed a rod underneath to keep my head from being crushed. Across the field we went, the car in reverse, dragging me. I hung on for dear life because the front tire would have immediately ridden over me if I had let go.

The farmer finally stopped his car and looked over to where I should have been sitting.

"Doc, where are you?"

"I am underneath the car," I replied as I attempted to crawl out. I soon realized that my legs couldn't move.

The farmer pulled me from under the car. He was very upset. He had experienced some of the worst life can bring, being a survivor of the Bataan March.

"Go to the house and call the vet clinic," I calmly said to him. "The cattle will leave me alone. Also, call your neighbors and bring an ironing board out here. I will be okay."

The farmer accomplished all this, and with the help of neighbors I was placed on the ironing board and brought to the house. I was lying on the kitchen floor, where it was warm, when Dr. Doornink arrived from Orange City. Dr. Fisher arrived later.

"Now, what's going on with you?" asked Dr. Doornink.

I explained the situation. He took out a needle and began poking my legs. There was no feeling. I was paralyzed from the waist down and sent directly to a hospital in Sioux City.

Many tests and X-rays were done, but they couldn't find anything to explain my paralysis. I continued to lie in that bed, unable to move my legs or feel any needle pricks.

Then one day, a young orthopedic surgeon came in. He confidently said he knew what was wrong with me and predicted that in a few weeks I would be good as new.

"There is a big blood clot on your spinal cord," he said. "I have seen this once before in Chicago. A fireman was hit in the back by a fire hose, which formed a blood clot that put pressure on his back. Once your blood clot is absorbed, you will be fine, just like the fireman."

So we waited. Finally, one evening just before Christmas, the situation began to improve.

They adjusted me so I could sit up straighter to eat my supper. "Look," I said. "I can move my toes on both feet."

In a few days, I could move my legs. I was one happy camper. Definitely one of the better Christmases I can recall!

CHAPTER EIGHTEEN

Sometimes an Animal Can Be Dangerous

It doesn't matter how tame an animal is; its personality can change in a split second. In particular, animals react swiftly when they feel threatened or trapped.

Many times, our practice took the difficult and dangerous calls no one else would take—we were the ones clients knew they could call in an emergency. This chapter covers some of the warning signs we looked for during calls. I'll also share stories about the more dangerous cases we dealt with, by species and condition.

WHEN TO WATCH OUT

If you watch animals closely, you can usually tell when they do not want you around. An ordinary cow that has a calf or is about ready to give birth will become protective and may try to kill you if you come too close. Watch closely when approaching her pen or stall. If she puts her head up, flattens her ears, and looks straight down at you, you are in trouble.

A bull will look at you, paw the ground, and toss dirt around before he charges. If the bull is in a fairly good-sized pen and intends to do you harm, he will often stand sideways and look at you.

Look out, because he will whip around, charge you with his head up, and slam his head down when he gets close enough to injure you.

Stallions, geldings, and mules usually kick instead of charge. Everyone is afraid of being kicked. They leave plenty of room behind the animal, but it is the front legs that will really injure or even kill you. If a stallion or gelding looks straight at you, he intends to do you bodily harm. He will go up on his hind feet, then whirl so his front feet are in a position to strike you. He will hit you with his legs and feet as they go up, then strike you again as they come down.

In a large pen, mares with foals will run straight at you with their ears flat and mouths open. Just before they get to you, they will quickly turn and kick with their rear legs.

I raised a lot of foals on my little farm. One night, we were watching an older mare we thought was going to foal soon. She did, and my hired man, Lee Meier, and I were ready to assist her. We got the foal off and the navel disinfected before the mare whirled around. We were fortunate to get out of there alive and without any injury. Before that night, she had always been a gentle mare.

The maternal instinct to protect their foals seems to last about three days in a mare. But overall, you can't trust any female animal that has just had her young.

Hogs

NEVER GO IN WITH A SOW ALONE

Almost every farm in Northwest Iowa had pigs, so we vaccinated a lot of hogs each year. A hog is far more dangerous than a horse or a cow, especially an old sow with little pigs. They are big animals that can turn on you in a second. Many people have been injured or killed by sows.

One Sunday morning in the fall, I was out on calls when my wife contacted me on the radio. She told me a client had called about a sow that had farrowed the night before and didn't have milk for her piglets.

The farmer was headed out the door to church, so I would be at the farm alone. My wife told me the patient was the first sow in the pen on the west side of the hog building. The sow was lying up against the wall of a typical ten-by-twelve pen. The little pigs were working her over, trying to get milk.

My plan was to give the sow a shot right behind the ear with a 2.5-inch, 14-gauge needle on a syringe. I climbed over the wood-paneled fence and swiftly gave her the shot. She bolted up and immediately came after me. My, was she quick! I hadn't even had time to turn around before I was flying backward. She grabbed me by my left thigh, swung her head, and threw me on my back. In a flash, she was on top of me.

She was a big sow. Her face was up by mine. She was trying to bite me, slobbering all over my head. I was wearing light gloves, and I shoved my fist—syringe, needle, and all—down her throat. Then, I pulled my hand out of the glove, leaving it in her throat. She backed up, and I got on my feet and flew backward to the fence. She spit the syringe and glove out and came toward me, but I managed to get over the gate before she got me.

I was bleeding like a stuck hog from a gash in my left leg, about eight inches above my knee. I went to the truck to put on a bandage and a tourniquet.

When I got back in my vehicle, my wife was on the radio.

"Mr. Swets just called from church," she said. "Be careful with that sow. She is a mean one."

"I found that out," I answered. "You need to call the doctor. My leg will need to be sewn up."

Mary felt bad, but I assured her that I was okay.

I learned a good rule that day: Never go in with a sow alone. If you have to, carry a scoop, shovel, or wood panel to keep her from you…because they can move like a streak of lightning.

VACCINATING HOGS FOR THE FLU

It was routine for us to go to farms in the fall to treat hogs for flu. Pigs could weigh up to 200 pounds, and they would come into the hog house at night to stay warm. It would sometimes get too hot for them, and they would start coughing. In some of the pigs infected with influenza, that cough would develop into pneumonia.

Most of the time, we would treat the whole herd with medication in their water. But the individual pigs with pneumonia needed antibiotics. We could pick them out based on their rapid breathing. (We called them "thumpers" because of the way their sides would quickly move in and out.) The preferred injection site was behind the ear. We would mark the thumpers' backs with chalk, so we would know for sure which pigs needed to be treated again.

I went to this one farm to treat pigs with a bad case of the flu. There was a cement feeding floor with a split elevation outside the hog house. Part of the floor was six inches higher than the rest and had a sharp drop-off. I took my antibiotics, syringe, needles, and chalk to mark the treated pigs.

It was a cold day, so I was wearing a parka. I went in the pen, walked up to a sick pig, gave it a shot behind the ear, and marked it with a piece of chalk. I forgot about the six-inch drop-off, tripped, and fell flat on my back, cracking my head on the cement.

I don't know how long I was out, but I assume it was a short time. When I woke up, these 200-pound pigs were chewing on my shoes, pants, legs, and parka. If I had been unconscious longer, they would have eaten me alive.

Bulls and Steers

WATCH OUT, THAT BULL WILL GET YOU SOMEDAY!

Henry W. Kleinhesselink milked Holstein cows at his Grade-A dairy. One time, when I was out to his farm, I noticed the big bull acting up—raising a fuss, throwing dirt, and bellowing.

I warned Mr. Kleinhesselink to watch out for that bull. I was afraid it might go after him someday.

"Not as long as I have this dog," said Mr. Kleinhesselink, pointing to his large farm dog. "He will protect me. He hates that bull, and the bull hates him."

"Just be careful," I told him, "and take this as a warning: That bull is dangerous."

Sure enough, one morning after a rain a very excited Mr. Kleinhesselink called to say the bull was on a rampage. It was wrecking his farm, and he wanted me to come out and shoot it. He was so distraught he spoke in a mixture of Dutch and English.

I grabbed my .270 rifle and drove to the farm. Peter Bonthuis, one of my regular assistants, was with me. When we got to the farm, half the neighborhood was there, sitting in cars along the road and watching the bull perform.

The bull had been in a pen of heifers. As he did every day, Mr. Kleinhesselink fed the heifers in a feed bunk in the pen, accompanied by his dog. This time, the bull went after the dog, crushing the animal into a pulp. There was hardly anything left of the dog. Mr. Kleinhesselink felt fortunate to have gotten out of the pen alive and unharmed.

The bull was now master of the farm—and he had gone mad. He had broken through a fence and was in a yard with the cow herd.

He stood on a little elevated spot east of the barn. Then he bellowed, put his head and neck under the cows' feed bunk, tossed it up into the air, and wrecked it.

Mr. Bonthuis drove our pickup to the north side of the barn. We both got out and walked to the fence. The bull paused in his destruction. With his head up high, he turned sideways and looked at us.

My intention was to rest the rifle on the fence post and shoot the bull in the head, which would save the meat for the family. Before I could get the rifle on the fence post, the bull came charging. As I looked through the rifle's scope, the bull got bigger and bigger.

I had to wait for the bull to drop his head. When I pulled the trigger, the bull dropped dead instantly, with his legs sprawled out. His stomach contents flew all over our legs, from the knees down.

That bull got too close for comfort. Mr. Bonthuis and I agreed that if we were ever in this situation again, we were going to stay in the pickup and do our shooting from there.

HOW MANY SHOTS CAN A BULL TAKE?

After a severe thunderstorm, Eugene Te Grotenhuis called me about his rampaging bull. He sounded agitated and asked me, "Can you come out right away, before he destroys the whole farm?"

A friend of mine, Al Hancock, was planning to go on a big-game hunting trip to Africa with his .458 Winchester. So I invited him along to hunt a bull in Northwest Iowa, which proved to be *almost* as exciting as big-game hunting in Africa.

We hurried to the Te Grotenhuis farm, but the neighbors had once again beaten us there and were watching the powerful bull tear up the farmstead.

Mr. Te Grotenhuis told us the bull had been out in the pasture with the cows. "When I went out to do chores, he just appeared," he explained. "He immediately took after me, so I ran to the alleyway of the corn crib and climbed a tractor. When he started climbing the tractor, I took off running for the house. He followed me to the back door before turning away."

The bull was now pacing between the interior of the barn and the alleyway. It was rather comical, since the bull would push open the top half of the barn door, look out, and turn his head from side to side as if daring us, "Catch me if you can." Then he would go back in the barn. The door would close behind him, and we would hear him wreaking havoc. Mr. Te Grotenhuis was worried the bull might get in the milk house, where the bulk tank was full of milk.

Before calling us, Mr. Te Grotenhuis had called the butcher shop, so they would be on hand to take the bull into town and prepare the meat. Employees from the shop arrived in a truck with a hoist for lifting dead animals. Mr. Hancock and I had climbed into the box of the truck, which was stopped along the fence, when the bull came out of the barn. He walked slowly along the fence, keeping his eyes on us all the time. I knew it would only be a matter of seconds before he charged.

I instructed Mr. Hancock on where to shoot the bull in the neck when the animal was broadside to us.

Mr. Hancock shot—but rather than go down, the bull came charging at us full speed. The air was filled with the sound of gunfire as we both shot at the bull. But the bull kept coming. He finally dropped right as he reached the end gate of the truck. I jumped out of the truck box to take a look.

The driver from the butcher shop also got out with a butcher knife to bleed the bull. As the driver came around the truck, the bull suddenly stood up. I still had my rifle, and I shot the bull right behind the head from a sideways distance of three feet. This time, the bull went down permanently.

It had taken seven shots to bring down that bull. The first shot had just grazed the top of the bone in the bull's neck. The other five shots went through his skull into his brain. Both eyes had been shot out. The final shot went into the neck bone, where it joins the skull.

The power of an adult bull can be amazing. No wonder oxen were trained to do farm work.

Mr. Hancock and I joked that there wasn't any need to go to Africa to hunt for big game. It could be found right here in Northwest Iowa.

HELP, THERE IS A BULL IN MY BASEMENT!

One day, Al Woudstra came running in the back door of the clinic. He worked at the butcher shop with his father, James, and brother, Lee. They needed me to come to the shop immediately with my rifle. (Our office was within a hundred feet of the shop.)

They had shot a Holstein bull that had been brought in for butchering. It went down in the chute like it was supposed to. They opened the chute, and the bull rolled out on the floor. That, too, was normal. They were about to start the butchering process, but before anything could be done the bull stood up.

That was *not* supposed to happen.

The bull ran out the door of the slaughter room, jumped over the stair railing, and then careened into the basement, where the cooling equipment for the freezers was located. The bull was mad and began wrecking things.

So I went down into the basement with my .270 and killed the bull.

A STEER STORY

When steers escaped, they often weren't recaptured immediately. If that happened, they would revert to being wild. In late summer, they could hide pretty well in a cornfield. But there was one problem: There usually wasn't any water in the cornfields for them to drink.

One farmer had an escaped steer that would exit the cornfield at sunrise and come down to the farm yard for water. The steer was wary, and he would stand at the edge of the cornfield to check if it was safe for him to come out.

To get that steer, I went out to the farm at three o'clock in the morning. I waited for the steer to come into range from an open haymow door, where I had a clear view of the water tank and cornfield. (The farmer had moved the water tank closer to the haymow, so the steer would have a longer distance to walk.)

The steer came real quietly and stood in the cornfield, where I could just make out his head. He was looking the situation over. Finally, the steer walked out to the water tank, and I shot him.

Dogs

WILD DOGS ON THANKSGIVING

The closest call I ever had with death came on a Thanksgiving Day.

Four inches of snow had fallen the night before. I received a call from a farmer southwest of Maurice, in Plymouth County. He and his family would be gone to Grandma's until four o'clock, he said; if I showed up around then, they would be home to help me treat their sick steer.

Other calls came that day. Someone else southwest of Maurice needed veterinary expertise. After I finished with that call, I headed to the farm with the sick steer. I knew I was early, but it didn't make sense to go elsewhere.

I parked my truck by the house yard. My whistling stopped when I opened my door and heard the most awful noise coming from the west side of the barn, where the pigs were housed. I was accustomed to pigs squealing, but this had a terrified ring to it. I wondered to myself, *Now what is going on?*

As I walked around the barn, the terrible noises grew louder. I knew whatever I found wouldn't be good; yet nothing could have prepared me for the horrific sight I beheld.

When I stepped around the corner of the barn, I observed a temporary pig pen the farmer had set up. It held about forty or fifty head of fifty-pound Hampshire pigs. I saw three large, white German Shepherds in that pen, covered with blood.

They were gripped in a killing frenzy. It didn't matter what or who—they only wanted to kill.

The pen was full of dead and dying pigs. The few live pigs were running around with many open wounds and their intestines hanging out. The dogs were just ripping the pigs apart.

I was less than six feet from one of the dogs. He was lying down, looking directly at me with murder in his eyes. That's when I made a terrible mistake. Instead of just backing away slowly, I waved my arms and yelled in a commanding voice, *"Get out of here!"*

The dog snarled, baring his teeth. He laid his ears back and started to get up. The hair on his back was standing on end, and it was clear he was in a killing mood. He growled again.

The barn doors and windows were shut. There was no way to escape. I knew I had made a mistake that could cost me my life. That dog would be on me in no time at all, and the other two would join him.

Suddenly, a group of pigs ran in front of the angry dog. Quick as lightning, the dog pounced on his prey. That gave me an opportunity to escape. I quickly stepped around the corner of the barn and made my way as fast as I could to the truck, leaving the dogs with the pigs and wishing I had brought a gun along.

As I debated what to do, I remembered being at this farm earlier in the month. The farmer's twin boys had been cleaning pheasants, so that meant there had to be a gun around. There was a simple lock on the porch that easily broke when I kicked the door in. Two double-barrel shotguns were on the porch, along with twelve-gauge shotgun shells. I loaded one of the shotguns, grabbed a supply of shells, and went back to the carnage.

I stopped at the corner of the barn and took aim. The first dog in my sights never knew what hit him.

Another shot hit dog number two in the belly as he was jumping a hog panel. He ran dying around the house, bleeding all over the fresh snow.

I quickly reloaded. The third dog also jumped the hog panel, heading west into a cattle yard. I waited to shoot until the dog had run through the yard and was trying to jump another fence. The shot hit him in the back, wounding him. He couldn't use his hind legs, but he continued moving through the cornfield. I went back to my truck and drove down the road, where he would come out. I killed him there, threw him on my truck, and went back to the farm yard.

Meanwhile, the family had come home. They were shocked to see blood outside on the snow all around their house. They also noticed the house had been broken into and that one gun was missing.

They listened while I quickly explained what had been happening when I arrived.

While assessing the damage, the family soon realized the dogs had not only caused havoc in the pig pen, they had also attacked the three 4-H calves belonging to the twin boys. The calves were cut up, but some fancy sewing remedied that, so they were still able to be shown at the Plymouth County Fair next July.

There was a shelter for sheep in the back of the grove. The dogs killed many sheep, and more had to be put to sleep because their injuries were too severe to hope for recovery. The dogs were fired up after that, continuing their killing spree in the pig pen. They wouldn't have quit until they had torn every pig apart.

I knew I easily could have been another one of their victims. It would have been a horrible way to die. But by the grace of God, a handful of pigs diverted the killers' attention.

From that day on, I always carried a gun in my truck.

I CAN'T TAKE THE DOG TO TOWN

One of my clients had recently retired from farming. As many farmers did, they had sold their farm and were making plans to move to town. They had a big German Shepherd, a good watch dog. But the dog couldn't move with them to town, nor could the farmer give him away because of the dog's meanness.

The family made an appointment for me to come out to the farm early one morning to put the dog to sleep. Albert Schuller, one of my helpers, came along.

The dog was tied to the farm yard's light pole with a chain approximately fifty feet long. He was standing erect, the chain taut, growling at us.

"Can you catch your dog and hold him by the collar?" I asked the farmer. "Al will then take the dog and hold it while I administer the shot." Because the farmer was quite elderly and not as husky and strong as Mr. Schuller, I wanted Al to hold the dog by the collar.

The dog suspicioned something was up and retreated to the pole. The farmer did get hold of the dog and started exclaiming—half in Dutch, half in English—to quickly come help him.

Al went to help. Just as he got there, the dog escaped from the owner's grasp. In an instant, he took off after Al.

Al immediately began running. Now, Al was a tall, well-fed farmer in his sixties. The dog was snapping his jaws and yipping at Al's behind.

The scene had the look of a cartoon. Al's legs were jutting out in front, his head and spine leaning back and his behind pushed forward. The dog was right on his rear.

The farmer was running behind the dog, reassuring Al in his broken Dutch/English, "I have insurance! I have insurance!"

The dog came to an abrupt stop when he reached the end of the chain.

"Did he bite you?" I asked Al.

"No," he replied. "I didn't know I could run that fast!"

Somehow, we managed to get the job done.

Horses

THAT DRAFT HORSE IS FURIOUS

I don't remember the client's name, but one Fourth of July I got a call from a local family. They wanted me to come to their farm to examine a draft horse.

The history of the case was as follows: The farmer had gotten the team of two horses up from the pasture the night before. He had hitched them to the mower they used to mow the road ditches around their farmstead. They were planning a big picnic with all their relatives, so the farmer had decided to clean up the place a little using the team.

When he was done, he put the team into their stall in the barn, fed them, and left them there overnight.

In the morning, he fed them a little grain. After they had finished eating, he stepped in between them to turn them out of the stall. Quick as a flash, one horse bit him through his overalls and shirt, tearing a piece right out of his abdominal area. He was fortunate to have gotten out of the stall with his life, because the horse had turned vicious and bit its teammate a number of times before that horse could break its halter and get away.

The farmer was, of course, in the hospital having his abdomen repaired. They had a large barn, with the whole north side made up of one pen. Cautiously, I approached the vicious horse, which was still in the stall. He just acted like he was sleepy. But when I got close, he woke up and tried to bite me.

To get the horse out of the stall, we cut the rope with an axe and kept our distance. He walked into the large indoor pen on the north side of the barn. We closed the gate. There, he was confined in a solid structure he could not escape. I told the family the symptoms indicated the horse probably had rabies.

He didn't want to eat or drink; he just stood there with his head down. I could see he could not swallow. If he had rabies, he would be down by the next day, unable to get up. We could destroy him and send his head to Ames to have his brain examined for the diagnostic evidence of rabies.

I warned the family not to let anyone in the barn and not to mess with this animal. I went back to the office and told Dr. Fisher about the case. He had never seen a horse with rabies, so he said, "Let's go out and take a look at it."

We went back to the farm. We peeked in between the boards on the side of the barn. The horse was standing with his back to the walk-in barn door. Along his left side was the stall fence, where they had partitioned off the barn with four-inch-thick creosoted posts and planks about six feet high. The horse's left side was against this plank partition, and his rump was against the door.

We knew we would have to be real careful, as this horse could fly into a rage if we touched him.

We found a bamboo fishing pole hanging on the side of the corn crib. Carefully, we opened the top of the walk-in door, just enough to slide the fishing pole into the stall. With the pole, we tapped the left side of the horse's neck.

He suddenly turned his head and bit the top off one of the four-inch creosoted posts. We slammed the door shut and locked it.

The next morning, the horse went down in the stall. I shot him in the neck. I removed his head, placing it in a washtub before transporting it by car to the laboratory in Ames.

The horse was diagnosed with rabies.

Rabies

RABIES DESCRIBED

There are two types of rabies: dumb and furious. The dumb form is the most common. The animal is lethargic and can hardly move. On the other hand, in the furious form the animal will bite, fight, and charge sources of movement or light. The common symptom between the two is that the affected animal will not drink water because it cannot swallow.

Any animal can have both forms of rabies. Skunks commonly harbor the rabies virus. I have also seen a number of dogs and cats with rabies. But in my lifetime, I have only seen five rabid horses.

Testing for rabies was almost always done at the lab at Iowa State, but for a time there was a laboratory in Sioux Falls that also did testing. The highway patrol would aid in getting small animals or animal heads to the lab, especially if there had been human exposure and a diagnosis was needed quickly. Patrolman to patrolman, the specimen was relayed, ensuring it got to the laboratory in one day.

Rabies is a serious disease. The virus travels up the nervous system until it reaches the brain. At this point, symptoms will finally manifest. If a bite is close to the head, symptoms will appear more quickly than if the bite is in a lower extremity, like a leg. There is still no successful treatment of rabies after it has reached the brain.

OVER THE TELEPHONE DIAGNOSIS

One evening, when I was at home, I got a call from a person in South Dakota. I was very surprised, as I didn't know them from Adam's off ox. (But, they had probably heard that I knew a little bit about horses.)

They said they'd had a veterinarian check their horse because it appeared to be sick. The veterinarian couldn't find anything wrong with the animal. Their description of symptoms led me to believe the horse could be suffering from the dumb form of rabies. In examining the animal, all parties had been exposed to saliva because the horse was drooling and could not swallow.

I told them that, based on what I was able to learn over the telephone, I thought there was a possibility the horse had rabies. I also told them that if the animal died or they put it down, they had to have the brain checked at the state laboratory.

A week later, they called to inform me the animal had died and laboratory tests were positive for rabies. They were being proactive. All those exposed to the animal's saliva were beginning a series of rabies shots.

A SLOBBERING HORSE

One summer, a woman who lived in Peterson called about her horse. Upon examining the horse, I suspected it had the dumb form of rabies. When the owner said the horse wanted to drink but could not swallow, I became more positive in my diagnosis.

I told her the horse probably had rabies and would soon die. I explained to her that the diagnosis could be confirmed if she sent the horse's brain to the state laboratory. She had been in contact with the saliva when she touched the horse's mouth. So if the animal had rabies, she had been exposed. As we were talking, the horse slung his head sideways, throwing saliva all over my right hand.

After the animal died, the laboratory confirmed it had rabies. I called the rabies hotline to determine what we had to do, since we had both been exposed. They recommended the horse owner take three vaccinations, but said I only needed two because I was up to date on the pre-exposure rabies vaccinations recommended for veterinarians. I didn't want to die of rabies, after all!

A RABID CAT

It was a Saturday afternoon in August, just before school started. I happened to be home for lunch when I took a call from Warren Kleinwolterink, who lived a couple miles north of town.

His family was packed and ready to leave on a vacation to the Black Hills. He had a sick cow he wanted me to look at before they took off. I went to their farm immediately. When I drove up to the barn, Mr. Kleinwolterink met me at the barn door. As I went in to see the cow, I stepped over the sill and saw a half-grown, gray cat lying there dead.

In passing, I told Mr. Kleinwolterink that he must have cat distemper on the premises. It was common for cats to have that disease in late summer and early fall.

"I hadn't seen that cat for a couple of days," he said. "It was the funniest thing when it came here sick. My son and the neighborhood kids, my wife, and I tried to feed him by hand. He even bit me, right through my thumbnail."

Sure enough, he had a beautiful blue ring around the spot where the cat had bitten through his nail.

I treated the cow before turning her out.

"We want to take our trip to the Black Hills," Mr. Kleinwolterink said. "I feel better now the cow has been treated. The neighbor is going to do the milking, and I didn't want to leave him with a sick animal."

I said I was going to send the cat to the laboratory to find out if it had rabies.

"Oh, I am sure it doesn't," he said.

Still, I insisted. My wife's brother was dating a girl from Orange City named Hazel Huisman. (She later became his wife.) He was going to stay with us that weekend so he could visit her, and I knew I could send the cat back with him to Ames.

On Sunday, when I saw my brother-in-law, I told him about this cat I had on ice and wanted to send back with him.

"Don't mess around," I said. "You take it in right away on Monday morning."

Later that morning, I got the call. The cat tested positive for rabies.

Time had lapsed since the family had been exposed. They needed to start their vaccinations immediately, which at that time were fourteen injections in the abdominal tissue. But the family had left on vacation, so the problem was finding them and bringing them back home. All we knew was that they were in the Black Hills. Even the neighbor didn't have a phone number to reach them.

Various law enforcement organizations were notified about finding this family, which they did. Needless to say, the family had to cut their vacation short to come back home and undergo rabies vaccination. In addition to the family, several other adults and some of the neighborhood children had been exposed to this cat. They all had to undergo vaccination, too.

I learned something very important from this experience: There is no such thing as luck.

Let's think about it. If you want to call it luck, it was lucky that the cow was sick. Otherwise, the family would have gone on their trip and I never would have been called. It was lucky Mr. Kleinwolterink wanted me to look at the cow before he left. Many people would have just gone on vacation and left the sick cow for the person doing chores. It was lucky the cat died just in front of the barn sill. It was lucky that when I stepped inside the barn, I saw the dead cat and mentioned it to the farmer, who then gave me the cat's history. Then, it was down to luck that my brother-in-law was in Orange City and could take the cat back to Ames, which saved time in the diagnosis.

Clearly, I never thought this could possibly all be luck.

CHAPTER NINTEEN

A Veterinary Clinic Grows

I owe my success, whatever it might have been, in large part to my employees. I was very fortunate to have good help when I was operating my practice. My employees were always willing to work long days, taking a call whenever it came.

I look at practices today and see they have strict hours and days of operation. Some practices offer no services on holidays and weekends. That doesn't match up with my line of thinking. Livestock doesn't watch the clock or the calendar; animals can have problems any time, day or night. Veterinarians need to be flexible and prepared to handle unexpected calls.

We offered twenty-four-hour service, seven days a week. I found, after all my years of practice, that people did not abuse this privilege. Many calls came in at four or five o'clock in the morning, when milking began, and at night when the farmers came in from the field. But whatever the time, when animals needed care clients asked for and received it.

TOP-NOTCH EMPLOYEES

In my practice, I appreciated all my employees. Several excellent veterinarians worked for me, many for a few years before they left to open their own clinic or work for an established practice they could buy into.

As I related in a previous chapter, I had a partnership with Dr. Robert Fisher early on in my career. The long hours and hard work took their toll on Dr. Fisher. He was worn out when he quit the practice in 1963. We'd had a perfect partnership of almost fourteen years. We got along well and never had a bad word between us.

Dr. Martin Van Der Maaten was the veterinarian in nearby Alton. He was fourteen years older than Dr. Fisher. In 1957, he joined Fisher and Neumann as a third partner. After he had a heart attack in the early 1960s, he retired from the practice.

A year later, his son, Martin Van Der Maaten, Jr., graduated from veterinary college in Ames. He also became a partner. After a few years, he decided to go back to college to study virology. Later in his career, he worked for the USDA. Many of his works in virology were published.

Due to the loss of these men, I began hiring recent grads. And for a short time, Dr. Larry Royer was my partner. After he left in 1974, I preferred to operate as a sole proprietor.

I can't say enough about the top-notch employees who worked for me. They came from Iowa State and Pennsylvania Vet College in Philadelphia. Some also came from Kansas State and Oklahoma State, along with a couple from Illinois.

To assist my veterinarians, we always employed two additional men to perform work on calls and around the practice. They would help with spraying livestock for parasites like lice and lend a hand when we needed an extra man while working with cattle or hogs. They helped with dehorning, transporting chutes, and keeping the equipment clean and in good repair. Barney Zigtema and Albert Schuller were full-time employees. Bob Bonnecroy was part-time.

My equine practice was growing, and so I employed an old horseman, Peter Bonthuis, to take care of the horses on my farm and go with me on equine calls. He worked for me until he was ninety-three years old.

Mrs. Betty Van Marel was the office secretary when I joined Dr. Fisher. She did excellent work and was employed until 1963. Mr. Ed Reinders then became the office manager. He was a very good office man and retired in the late 1970s. Mr. Cliff Mouw had just retired from farming, so he came onboard and worked for me until the practice closed in 1979.

There was only one man I had to fire.

He was an Iowa State grad and a good practitioner. Yes, he was good. But he was giving me trouble because he didn't always want to take farm calls.

One day, some of the boys were sitting in the back room, talking and having lunch. I could hear this man talking about my wife. She had sent him on a call the evening before, but he had given her trouble. He didn't go, so the farmer called her back. She assured him she would get a vet out to his farm. So, she called this young man again. I heard him tell the boys, "I really told her off."

I stepped into the room. His back was toward me, so he kept talking. The other vets could see me and looked quite uncomfortable. I told this man to leave his keys, collect his pay, and leave immediately.

OUR CLIENTS

Most of our clients were located around Alton, Granville, Hospers, Orange City, Peterson, Sioux Center, and Sutherland. All our veterinarians worked out of the Orange City office except Dr. Royer. He lived in Ireton and worked from his home. We all assisted him with western Sioux County clients.

We treated all the breeds and types of animals you can find on a farm, including poultry. Everyone helped with all types of cases, but the elder Dr. Van Der Maaten did most of the small animal work.

Most farms were diversified, keeping pigs, chickens, sheep, goats, cattle, dairy cows, and horses. A farmer was a big operator if he kept 1,000 head of cattle or 200 or 300 pigs. Dairies, on the other hand, were small. I would imagine the biggest dairy was somewhere around 100 to 150 cows.

TWO-WAY RADIOS

Soon after I began working with Dr. Fisher, we purchased two-way radios. We were the first veterinarians in the state of Iowa to install them. And in those days, the FBI had to come and investigate before a business could connect a two-way radio system.

Once the radios were installed, we thought we were on top of the world because they saved us a lot of driving. Prior to the radio system, the office would call clients and ask them to tell the veterinarians where their next stop would be. If no one was in the house to answer the phone or if we had already left, we had to go back to the office to figure out where the next call was. Sometimes, we had to head right back to the area we'd just left.

The radios were also installed in our homes, so when our wives answered the phones after office hours it was much easier for them to locate a veterinarian and get them to the client.

With the two-way radios, we could talk to Hawarden, Sioux City, Sioux Rapids, and Spencer. When on the fringes of the practice territory, we had to find an elevated point to connect with the master station in the office, which had a 93-foot tower.

It worked real well. I furnished everyone with their own vehicle and radio. We kept updating them as new models were released.

When I closed my practice, the radios were obsolete. By that time, we had exchanged them for cell phones—which were much larger than they are today!

THE TELEPHONE OFFICE

When I came to Orange City, the telephone office was staffed by a switchboard operator twenty-four hours a day. Most of the operators were women. If I wanted to make a phone call, I would first call the telephone office and give the operator the number of the party I wanted to call. She would ring them up. There was no direct calling. Our office number was 276.

The country lines were still party lines. That meant several farm families were on the same telephone line. Each farm had a different ring. For example, one family's ring might have been two longs and one short. That's how you knew you were being called, though everyone on the party line could listen in.

In the first years I practiced in Orange City, we got a lot of nighttime calls to deliver calves and pigs. When a call came in at night, the telephone operators could listen in and figure out where Dr. Fisher and I were. If another call came in, they would let our wives sleep and call the farm we were currently working at. At 7:00 a.m., they changed operators.

Our downtown office was next to the telephone office. When they switched operators in the morning, we often gave the girls a ride home. (We would also bring coffee and bakery treats for them.)

CARS AND STATION WAGONS

We kept up with the newest innovations, and that included eventually exchanging cars for station wagons.

The cars did their best, but the gravel roads were hard on them. When I came to Orange City, K64 north of town and

Highway 10 to Granville were still gravel. I purchased a new six-cylinder Ford around the first of December 1951, but by the first of June it was a total wreck. It had been a snowy winter. There were big drifts on the corners, so when the snow melted in the spring the gravel roads were full of potholes and ruts. The cars got stuck and often needed pulling out. In those first years, farmers usually used horses to pull me and other motorists out when we were stuck.

I drove my Ford and Dr. Fisher drove a Studebaker Champion. Later, we both changed to Pontiac station wagons. We bought our first ones in Sioux Center, and later at the Even car dealership in Alton. They were built heavier than our old cars and could take the abuse of rural roads.

DAILY LOG

I kept a daily log of farm stops and services performed. Here is an example from September 8, 1963:

> *Horses*
> *Feedlot heifer*
> *Dairy cows*
> *Sows*
> *Steers*
> *Deliver a calf, already there, $3.50*
> *Examine cattle*
> *Cut two bulls, $6.50*
> *Castrate pigs, 1 bull, $5.50*

My biggest day on record was fifty calls, for which I drove over 500 miles. Peter Bonthuis, who was seventy years old at the time, would help me in the morning and Al Schuller would help in the afternoon. When K64 was first blacktopped, it did not have a posted speed limit. I often drove 70 miles an hour, putting 90,000 miles a year on my practice vehicle.

My wife would usually call and let me know when supper was ready. Too many times I had to tell her I still had two or three farm calls to finish. I now wish I would have been able to spend more time with the family. Most nights, I would come home, eat a bit, shower, and fall asleep until the alarm sounded.

I liked the variety of work and treating multiple animal species. I think this type of practice made me sharper at making a diagnosis and prescribing a treatment. When you have a large practice, you learn quickly what treatments are successful and which ones have little effect.

OPERATING CLINIC OPENS

Around 1958, Dr. Fisher and I hired Kepp Construction to build a facility on the southern edge of town. When it was done, we had stalls, an operating table, and a sterile environment for large animal surgery. We referred to this building as our "clinic on the highway." The small animals and office work remained uptown.

In those days, we operated on a lot of cattle to treat "hardware disease." Cows would eat pieces of wire or nails, which would puncture one of their four stomachs. The animals would become sick, and we would operate to take the metal objects out. It was much better and much easier to do this surgery in the clinic than out on the farm.

The stalls allowed us to provide professional aftercare for as long as the animal needed it. There were also heated kennels with outside runs for boarding dogs and other pets. We held an open house when the building was done, inviting farmers and other veterinarians to tour the new facility.

DISEASE-FREE PIGS

About 1960, we built an addition to the clinic on the highway where we could raise disease-free pigs. The most prevalent disease we needed to prevent was rhinitis. By raising young pigs in a sterile environment and then placing them on farms that had been cleared of diseases, they would remain healthy.

A client would bring healthy-bred gilts ready to farrow to the butcher. The sow was killed, and we would quickly perform a cesarean to remove the baby pigs from the uterus under sterile conditions. The piglets were then transferred to our disease-free facility. Because they never came in contact with other sows or hogs, the pigs didn't have a chance to pick up rhinitis.

The baby pigs were fed with nipples on an automatic feeder. At a certain age, they were moved to the clients' facilities, which had been cleaned and disinfected.

Mr. Bob Van Roekel was in charge of this part of the practice as long as we had it. He did an excellent job.

TREATING CHICKENS

I was always invited in for lunch, dinner, or supper wherever I was working. As a rule, I often accepted the invitation and found it a great way to get to know people.

If the veterinary work was satisfactory, you often began to work for clients' relatives; that was particularly true of my Dutch and German clients, as they were very close-knit families. I also noticed that if you made a good impression on the wife, you would be called to do veterinary work more often. Many times, when I had been out to a farm to look at some other livestock, the wife would come out and say, "Doc, come have a look at my chickens, please."

Almost all farms had chickens, and farm wives depended on the money from egg sales for groceries and other items. I can think of six businesses on Main Street that dealt in poultry, selling baby chicks and/or buying eggs. In fact, when I came to Orange City, one of the selling points for the new cars that came out each fall was how many egg crates would fit in the trunk. The salesman had egg crates right there to demonstrate.

Both Dr. Fisher and I were reasonably good at treating sick poultry, and rarely did we charge for the medicine. For conditions or diseases we couldn't take care of, we told clients to call the hatchery to treat their flock.

DEHORNING

It was common for dairy and beef animals to have horns in the early days of my practice. Dr. Fisher didn't do any dehorning—and neither did anyone else—so the work often fell on my shoulders. When people realized I could dehorn cattle, the calls started coming in. So, we purchased a dehorning chute with an attached head gate and table.

Mike Te Grotenhuis was the first man I hired to help me with dehorning. Later, Bob Bonnecroy and Bob Van Roekel assisted me. We worked well together as a team. One of them would get the animal into the chute, the other would close the head gate, and I would do the cutting. Al Schuller and Barney Zigtema also helped on many dehorning calls.

Once, at a farm near Hospers, we had 450 Hereford feeder calves to dehorn, weighing about 450 pounds each. The farmer's elderly father sat there with a pocket watch. Later he told us, "When you started out, you were doing a calf every seven seconds. Now it takes five seconds."

It's doubtful anyone else could be faster than our team when we were working like clockwork!

DO SOME GOOD THING

One of my best moments as a veterinarian came after I had my first bad car accident. I was lying in the hospital on Sunday; little did I know I was also being discussed next door at First Reformed Church.

"A lot of you folks have Doc Neumann as your veterinarian," said the Reverend Dr. Henry Colenbrander from the pulpit. "He had a bad accident earlier this week. It would be a good thing if you all went over to the hospital to say hello!"

Many of them came to see me, including the Reverend Dr. Colenbrander—a short, fiery man, who came to visit every day while I was in the hospital. He wasn't my pastor, but I always liked him.

He told me, "The Lord has saved you to do some good thing."

I brushed his words off at the time, but they did come back to me over the years.

The Sioux Veterinary Clinic prepares for Orange City's Centennial.

This property was purchased in 1954 to construct a new clinic. The business changed its name to Sioux Veterinary Clinic in 1959.

This building contained a large, modern operating room, a recovery room, and dog kennels. It was located on Highway 10.

Photos courtesy of *The Centennial Book: Orange City, Iowa, 1870-1970*, printed by the Ad-Visor. Centennial Book Production Staff: Rev. E. Van Engelenhoven, Editor; Harvey Pluim, Publisher; Edward Stetson, Design; Fred Brandes, Composition; and Keyron Shumacher, Pressman.

192 | A Veterinary Clinic Grows

This log book kept track of farm visits, charges, and payments.

Another busy day at the office.

CHAPTER TWENTY

Just What Is Going On?

I can laugh about it now, but it was not so funny at the time. What happened in the late 1970s caused a lot of stress for both me and Mary Virginia.

SICK CATTLE

As a practice, we were driving 90,000 miles a year on each of our four vet trucks. We had a tremendous customer base.

The northwest corner of Iowa was home to many farms, most of which had cattle, dairy cows, and swine. There were days we vaccinated over a thousand cattle. I had a large cooler where I could store a quantity of vaccine, thereby allowing me to purchase vaccines at bulk prices. It made sense to purchase 27,000 doses of rhinotracheitis vaccine (we called it "red nose vaccine") from a salesman we had done business with for many years. I had to buy the diarrhea virus vaccine separately. Together, these vaccines were used as a preventative for the disease complex often called "shipping fever."

The vaccines had worked well for years. But suddenly, almost every herd we vaccinated began getting sick a week to ten days after they had been treated.

We sent blood and tissue samples to the state laboratory in Ames; they could not give us a diagnosis or cause of the problem. From the cattle's symptoms, it appeared they had the diarrhea virus.

When the lab could not give us a diagnosis or cause, we sent more blood and tissue samples to the federal laboratory north of Ames. This was done several times. We even sent a veterinarian to discuss the problem with the lab. But we still didn't get any answers.

Time passed. I vaccinated 750 yearling cattle belonging to a very good client of mine. Exactly one week later, some animals in the herd became sick. They were off their feed, refusing to eat and carrying a two- to three-degree fever.

I was desperate to find an answer. So, I purchased a sick steer from my client and hired his son to take it down to the state laboratory. (I needed all my help to run the 750 steers through the chute and give antibiotics to those with a temperature.)

The steer was sent to Ames with instructions not to treat it, but to let the condition run its course. We also asked that they perform any tests or procedures that would enable them to diagnose the disease and its cause.

I also notified the federal lab that we had a steer at the state lab for observation. If that animal died, the lab in Ames was to send blood and tissue samples to the federal lab.

I made two other telephone calls, one to the head Iowa State veterinarian and one to the federal veterinarian for the State of Iowa. I told them I *had* to have an answer to the problem.

The steer died.

The cause of death was an infection of a certain strain of the diarrhea virus. According to reports sent to me, this strain of the virus was sent to the federal lab by the diagnostic lab at Iowa State. So, everyone knew the cause of the steer's death.

THE ANSWER

A representative of the federal lab came to my office approximately a week after we all received the results. I came in from work one evening, and this individual was waiting in my office. He wanted to talk about the death of the steer.

On paper, he had a list of lot numbers of diarrhea virus vaccine that had been manufactured by a licensed laboratory in Omaha, Nebraska. He asked me if I had any vaccine or had had any vaccine with one or more of these numbers.

I went into the cooler and produced several samples of the vaccine bearing the lot numbers he had in hand.

He told me that somewhere along the line the vaccine manufactured in the plant had been contaminated with a lethal strain of diarrhea virus. The contaminated vaccine had then been released to various drug suppliers for sale. Inspections of the product had not been done correctly—if at all.

A recall was issued on the contaminated vaccines under the pretext the labels had not been properly developed and printed. But what was already in the hands of local veterinarians was not recalled. I had already bought 27,000 doses at a good price from my supplier.

Apparently, I was the only person who had bought a significant amount of the vaccine before the recall. No one bothered to inform me the vaccine was contaminated.

I don't remember the exact number of contaminated herds, but I think it was around twenty-seven. These farmers sustained a loss since the cattle did not gain weight, and some of the animals died. It was also labor intensive to treat these herds. The farmers were not happy.

When it was discovered the company had released the vaccine for sale and recalled it under false pretenses, the government rescinded their license. The company closed down. Many people lost their jobs. Some were innocent employees, while others were guilty government inspectors who had not done their jobs properly.

I began to get attention for my response to the situation. I received a telephone commendation from the head federal veterinarian of Maryland. I also somehow caught the attention of the Department of Internal Revenue Service and the Bureau of Animal Industry. (The Bureau was established in 1894 to promote livestock disease research, enforce animal import regulations, and regulate the interstate movement of animals.)

The good thing about this situation—if there is anything good—is that the owners of the affected herds came to my office and met with the former president of the vaccine manufacturing company. He reimbursed the livestock owners for any animals they lost, as well as loss of weight gain in the affected livestock.

The farmers' bills were all paid without question. My clients were compensated fairly well for the ordeal.

But our troubles were not over yet. We spent the next couple years paying the price of being a whistleblower.

On my end, I found I could no longer hire professional people. Somehow the word was spread, "Don't work for that guy in Orange City." I had to hire an attorney to defend myself against false allegations, leveled mainly on the health sheets. I was cleared of everything.

IRS SAYS NOW

One day, I was sitting in the chair getting a haircut at Lambert Hollinga's barber shop. As usual, there were a few men sitting in the chairs, waiting their turn.

Mr. Hollinga was half done with my haircut when a man dressed in a suit walked into the shop.

"Is there a Doc Neumann here?" he asked.

"That's me," I answered.

"I am from the Department of the Internal Revenue Service." He introduced himself, flashed some identification, and asked to see some papers regarding my income tax. He wanted to see them immediately.

"Once my haircut is finished," I said. "We will go over to my lawyer."

"I said *now*," he commanded.

I got up with my partially done haircut and took him to my attorney's office. After introductions, I went back to finish my haircut. It was rather embarrassing, as all the men in the barber shop knew me. Some were even my clients.

The IRS couldn't find anything wrong. My wife was an excellent bookkeeper. She had learned from her father, who was a Certified Public Accountant. The examinations by the IRS were grueling and tremendously hard on her.

There were weekly meetings with a representative from the IRS. He always requested more reports from her bookkeeping. When the preliminary paperwork was done, Mary met with a higher-up IRS official. Prior to this meeting, she was advised by our lawyer to dress simply and without jewelry. The only problem they could find was that we had depreciated some livestock too quickly, so we owed tax on that.

I figured they had to come up with something.

QUITTING MY PRACTICE

That episode led to me quitting my livestock practice. It was 1979. When the contracts I had with my veterinary employees expired, I let them go one by one. I sold my office building to a Chinese restaurant chain. Most of the medications and equipment were sold to two veterinarians in South Dakota.

This decision was hard on us. We sent out a letter informing our clients—many of whom were friends that had been with me from the start—that my general practice work at the Sioux Vet Clinic in Orange City was ending.

I was fifty-three years old. The children were in college or pursuing their careers. Mary and I were empty nesters.

Now what?

PART III

The Draft Horse Years

CHAPTER TWENTY-ONE

Belgian Draft Horses

In the letter I sent to my clients about the closure of my general practice, I announced that I was going to continue practicing veterinary medicine. My focus was going to shift to equine medicine. For the rest of their livestock needs, they would have to call another veterinarian.

GETTING STARTED

My office was now my truck. The equipment was pared down to the bare minimum of what I felt was necessary for my work, including the drugs I was most likely to use to treat horses.

I had always liked horses. When I was young, I used to ride with Dr. Roach. He treated all kinds of livestock. At that time, horses were used for both work on the farms and transportation, so keeping them healthy was a big part of his practice.

Horses were important to the Neumann family. My parents always had horses on their small farm, and my siblings and I always had a horse to ride. My dad's father had been a cavalryman in the Prussian army. So, one could say a love of horses ran in our blood.

I'd always longed to have my own team of good draft horses. Back in 1960, I bought a pair of mares from a Belgian breeder—Orville Pierce of Oakland, Iowa. He became one of my best friends, and he taught me quite a bit about the Belgian draft horse. Together, we went to many horse shows, parades, and clinics.

When I bought the team, one of the mares was in foal. I told Mr. Pierce I didn't want to raise foals, but I would buy the pair. Once the foal was weaned, Mr. Pierce would buy it back. The mare foaled, and her filly was weaned as planned. Then it was time for Mr. Pierce to come pick her up.

Men are entitled to change their minds, just like women. I had enjoyed the whole process of birthing and watching the little filly grow so much that I decided I wanted to raise and train Belgian foals.

It was good fun for Mary and me. Once I quit my general practice, we were both free to be out together after years of being tied down. She really liked the horses and would help with them when needed. She was happy to go on a buggy ride at night and enjoyed meeting and talking to people at horse shows.

QUALITY DRAFT HORSES

Interest in draft horses was growing. Arnold Hexom established the Waverly Horse Sale around 1948. It became one of the largest draft horse sales in the Midwest. My first yearlings were sold at one of Mr. Hexom's sales. We became good friends with him and his wife, Lorine.

Mary Virginia and I were also employed by Mr. Hexom in 1970. I did veterinary work and checked the health papers of the horses up for sale. Mary helped me with paperwork and worked in the sales office. We purchased a copy machine, which was a fairly unusual piece of office equipment at the time. Mary and I continued to work for Mr. Hexom when he moved his sale to the fairgrounds at Waterloo.

The state of Indiana also had a huge draft horse sale. There was a much better market there for registered Belgians. The horses I brought to the sale were absolutely ready to sell, trained and looking good. Consequently, they sold for top dollar.

The best compliment I ever received happened at one sale where I brought in fourteen head, all yearlings. They were fit perfectly, shod, and ready for the sale ring. A group of elderly Belgian horse breeders were studying the yearlings as they stood in a row in their stalls.

"You know, Doc, that is the best string of yearlings I have ever seen," one man said. "And I bet you one thing."

"What's that?" I asked.

"I bet you have the best ones at home yet."

He was right. I had kept the best three—a stud colt and two yearling fillies—at home. I tried to raise between ten and fourteen yearlings every year. At one time, I had forty-five head of registered Belgians—foals and breeding stock—on the farm.

DRAFT HORSE DOC

Because of my veterinary work with Mr. Hexom and at other horse sales, I got to meet many draft horse breeders. We went to a show or two a year. When the breeders realized I was a veterinarian, they often told me about their horses' health problems. Soon, I became known as the "Draft Horse Doc."

I rarely sold horses or stock directly off the yard. Instead, I took my yearlings and the older mares to sales. I wanted buyers and breeders to see my stock and see them sell. That way, the horses brought in more money and more recognition for me. If there was anything wrong with the animal ready for sale, I always called it. The buyers knew what they were getting. This helped me build a good reputation.

I had fifty acres of property on which I raised my horses. It was mostly pasture; only seventeen acres were crop land. I built one barn and moved another one in so there were adequate facilities for foaling my Belgian mares.

PETER BONTHUIS

When I bought that first pair of registered Belgian mares, I already had two saddle horses. Since I owned the drafts, I attracted the attention of an old horse buyer, Peter Bonthuis. (His Dutch last name, by the way, translates to "spotted house.")

Mr. Bonthuis had been a horse dealer for almost all his life. And he was extremely knowledgeable about the draft horse. I learned an awful lot from him about horse psychology, including how to handle horses in challenging conditions. I hired Mr. Bonthuis to help take care of my animals at the stables, and he would sometimes ride with me in the country when I was making horse calls.

His services were valuable. Everyone in the surrounding countryside knew Pete. Most of them had had business dealings with him in the past, when farmers had to rely on horse power. He was sharp, and together we did veterinary work on some horses that were just plain hard to handle. As I became more involved in the draft horse industry, I developed a large clientele and had the opportunity to treat problems most ordinary practitioners would never encounter.

Mr. Bonthuis was also a very talented draft horse showman. When he entered a horse into a show, he intended to win—not to take second or third, but *first* place. Occasionally, he would say to me, "Doc, we are here to win!"

Outside the show ring, Mr. Bonthuis was excellent at appraising people. He developed this talent during his years of horse trading.

Back in the Depression, Mr. Bonthuis sometimes only made a one-dollar profit per sale. He couldn't afford to lose *anything*, so he had to learn to read people. He could determine whether someone was trustworthy by observing their behavior and appearance—how they talked, how they looked at you, how they parted their hair. If we met a person who he deemed untrustworthy, he always told me to turn around and walk away. "You can't deal with them," he would say. "In the end, they will get you."

A FARM SALE EXPERIENCE

Let me tell you a story that demonstrates what a good judge of character Peter Bonthuis was.

There was a farm sale northeast of Le Mars. At the time, I was collecting antique farm machinery. There were several pieces of antique horse machinery on sale, and I decided to buy them. I sent Mr. Bonthuis and Barney Zigtema to the sale with my checkbook. That evening, when I got in from work, I called Mr. Bonthuis.

"We purchased them all," he said. "We brought home the machinery that would fit on the pickup. Tomorrow morning, we plan to go get the rest."

The next morning, Mr. Bonthuis and Mr. Zigtema were shocked to find the machinery was gone. They could not find it anywhere, and no one knew anything of its disappearance. They called me on the two-way radio to tell me about the missing merchandise, and I went down to the farm where the sale had been held.

Mr. Bonthuis said, "We can't find the rest of the machinery we bought. But Doc, I know who took it."

"How do you know?" I asked.

"Remember, Doc, when I told you there are people with certain attributes that mark them as untrustworthy? Well, there was a man at the sale who exemplified those attributes to a T. He was watching everything I bought," said Mr. Bonthuis.

"How are we going to find him?" I asked.

"I know he bought a mower, just four items down from this machinery you purchased," answered Mr. Bonthuis. "We will go to the bank. They will have a picture of the layout and will know exactly who bought the mower."

We went to the bank to inquire. They gave us the name and the address of this gentleman. He was a trucker who lived on an acreage west of Le Mars.

"We will drive over there," said Mr. Bonthuis. "We won't drive on the yard, but if we just drive by the place, perhaps we will see something."

Sure enough, there was our equipment, sitting right in the middle of the yard. We could see it from the road.

We went back to the sheriff's office in Le Mars. We told the sheriff that we were missing some items we had purchased from the sale…and where we had seen them. We also gave him a list of what had been taken.

The sheriff went to the place and talked to the man's wife, as the gentleman in question was gone for the day. The sheriff told her we would come in the afternoon to pick up what belonged to us and take it off the yard. And that *no one* was to bother us or disturb the equipment. The sheriff left an order that her husband was to be at his office at promptly nine o'clock the next morning.

The men working for me picked up the equipment from off his yard. The next morning, Mr. Bonthuis and I went to the sheriff's office. We arrived a little early and sat in the corner to wait for the trucker to join us.

"Doc, you be careful. This man is going to be late, and he is going to have a big story," advised Mr. Bonthuis. "He is going to ask you if you said he *stole* the equipment. Don't you say he stole it—you say he *took* it."

With that advice from Mr. Bonthuis in mind, we waited. It was about fifteen minutes later that we heard the gentleman come in the door.

"I was so busy this morning," the man said loud enough that we could clearly hear him. "I really hated that the equipment got messed up. I felt so bad about that."

The receptionist directed him into the office where we were sitting with the sheriff and deputies.

The man's eyes were cold and beady. I almost had a heart attack when I saw how perfectly he matched Pete's description of an untrustworthy person.

"So, this is Doc Neumann," he said. "You didn't say I *stole* it now, did you?"

"No, I didn't," I answered. "I just said you had it."

He turned to the sheriff. "I am so sorry about that equipment. The fellows there were loading this and that. I was tired. Just not paying attention. I felt so bad when I realized it was not my stuff."

Yes, I'm sure he did.

Our lives drastically changed when the office closed. But my work in the draft horse industry brought many great people into our lives...including Peter Bonthuis.

Grandfather Neumann's discharge papers from the Prussian cavalry.

One of the first pairs of purebred Belgian mares I raised. They were sold at a draft horse show and sale in Cedar Rapids, where they topped the market.

Lady Ann, ready for a show.

Peter Bonthuis with a pair of my Belgian mares.

Peter Bonthuis and I successfully robbed the bank of pennies a week before Orange City's centennial celebration to toss to children.

Photo courtesy of Katy Hansen, photographer.

This wooden Case threshing machine I found in North Dakota took six teams of horses walking in a circle to power it.

Several elderly men taught me to operate steam engines. They had used them in their farming practices.

I not only collected antique farm machinery, I also hosted and participated in demonstrations. I found this 80-horsepower steam engine in a logging camp in Minnesota. It had been abandoned, but my friend, Bill Tolman, and I restored it to operating condition.

CHAPTER TWENTY-TWO

Memories of a Horse Doc

After the close of my general practice, my reputation as a horse doc continued to grow. It didn't take long for horse owners all over Northwest Iowa—and in other parts of the country—to start asking me to examine their horses.

ANOTHER CAR ACCIDENT

In 1979, early in my horse-doctoring days, I was on my way to answer a farm call near Cherokee. It was around noon, and I was travelling on a blacktop road. Soon, a sign informed me there was road work ahead. The detour was a gravel road.

As I was driving down the gravel road, I saw two men coming out of a farm house. Almost immediately past the house, there was an unmarked four-way intersection.

A milk truck broadsided me at the intersection. My truck flew across the road, hitting a big utility pole before bouncing back into the intersection. What was left of my truck landed by the milk truck's cab, which was lying on its side in the middle of the intersection.

The vet box in my truck was totally destroyed. My veterinary supplies were scattered on the road and in the ditch. The cab of my truck was also destroyed, except where I was sitting. I was hanging out the back window of the truck, with my feet caught in what was left of the steering wheel.

The two men I had seen coming out of the house rushed down to the accident. They thought I was dead, so they proceeded to help the milk truck driver out of his cab. The men were afraid there was going to be a fire. Once the other driver was carried to a safer spot, they heard me make a noise. The men took me out of the wreckage and placed me in the ditch next to the other driver, where we waited for medical help.

I remember waking up in the ditch. I could see a pair of jeans on my left-hand side. Then, I saw this grayish mask in front of my face. I took my left hand, got underneath it, and put it on my head.

It was my scalp.

"Doc, you should not have done that," said one of the men.

I was about half-looped and said, "Why not? It is mine, isn't it?"

"Yes, it is. But it is full of gravel and grass."

Most of the ribs on my left side were broken. I also had plenty of bruises, besides being scalped. My truck and box were a total loss. The milk truck driver came out better. He just had a broken arm.

They took me to the Cherokee hospital, where they cleaned up my scalp and sewed it back on my head. Two days later, I was back to work. Still in my employ was a licensed veterinary assistant, Shane Kirschten, who did the driving and worked on the cases we went to see while I recovered.

That was a bad accident. There is a spot on the top of my head that never completely healed. When I go to a new barber, I am always asked about it.

DOCTORING FOR THE AMISH

As a horse doc, I did a lot of veterinary work for Amish farmers. The cases I worked on for them helped me develop effective treatments for two common equine ailments.

Tetanus in horses is common on Amish farms. I started thinking about better ways to treat tetanus. I assessed the disease and found drugs that would attack the symptoms. The two-week treatment I developed is a combination of vaccinations, medicine given intravenously, and pills. It is almost a hundred percent effective and will usually save the horse.

Green grass and too much grain can also founder a horse, and they are a pretty common occurrence on Amish farms. While this won't kill a horse, the resulting chronic lameness renders it useless. For this ailment, I was able to develop a treatment that is ninety-eight percent effective.

THE BEST JOB

Looking back, I would have to say the best and most prestigious job I was called to do as a horse doc was some equine work for the Caisson Platoon of the Third Infantry. The Third Infantry is the oldest outfit in the army and can trace its beginning to the Revolutionary War. The division buries their dead in Arlington Cemetery. There is a museum in Washington, D.C., dedicated to its history.

The year was 2007 or 2008. The Caisson Platoon asked me to come to Washington, D.C., to castrate thirteen horses. A gentleman—a rich man, I think—had donated these stallions to the outfit. Even though some were two or three years old, they still had to be castrated and trained. An army major, who was also a veterinarian, had begun the process. When the first horse stood up after the procedure, his intestines came out. He had ruptured. They got the horse down again and sewed him, but the horse still died. When this happened twice, the army stopped the castration.

They asked me to come, and I said sure. They treated me like royalty.

The troops picked me up from the airport. I stayed in an apartment in an area of the military district that was off-limits to enlisted personnel. (The Secretary of the Navy lives there when he is in town.) It was a little way from the city, on a hill where you can look over D.C. The apartment was sometimes used by visiting dignitaries. To a veterinarian from Iowa, it was plush! I took my meals in the mess hall with the troops.

The castration almost became a ceremony. All the local military brass was there to see the job done. And soldiers, too, so I had a lot of help. One major asked me how long it was going to take. I assured him I would be done by noon. He said he hoped so, as they all wanted to watch the game. (It was Super Bowl Sunday.)

I got to work. There were a couple of ruptures, but before I let the horses stand up I sewed them. I had very little trouble.

And yes, the work was done before noon.

Soldiers from the Third Infantry later took me through their museum, Arlington Cemetery, General Lee's house, and other points of interest in our nation's capital.

AN HONORARY MEMBER

The colonel in charge ordered the available soldiers into formation. In a short ceremony, he made me an honorary member of the Caisson Platoon. He gave me two caps and t-shirts that I have never worn. When this colonel retired, he invited me to come to his retirement celebration. After this several men from the platoon came to our horse clinics in Orange City.

Later on, the platoon had trouble training the horses. They asked me if I knew anyone on the East Coast who could help. I did not, but I knew someone in Iowa—Bob Mouw of Newkirk. Mr. Mouw trained the horses on his farm. Once he felt they were ready, he and his wife delivered the horses to the stables in D.C., where the horses were used at Arlington Cemetery.

This is the t-shirt that was presented to me. It was indeed an honor to work with Caisson Platoon.

A PRESIDENTIAL QUESTION

I once received a letter from President Jimmy Carter's secretary. His daughter, Amy, had a horse that appeared to have a blood wart. (A woman who worked in the president's office was from Sioux Falls. She had heard about me, so that's probably why they contacted me.)

I advised them to anesthetize around the spot. I said they should then cut it out and burn the spot with a hot iron. It's an old-fashioned treatment that works a hundred percent of the time. I never heard back from the Carters, but I did hear through the grapevine that the suggested treatment worked.

CHRISTMAS IN WESTFIELD

One year, in late November, I was called to a farm in Westfield. The farm was a rented place, and it was pretty worn down. There was just a mother and her young daughter living there. I would guess the daughter was nine or ten years old.

Their mare had a broken hind leg. The little girl was crying. This was her horse, and she thought I was going to put it down.

I looked at the mare, then at the little girl. I said we could put a splint on the mare's hind leg, but we would also have to put the patient in a sling. (A sling is used to keep a horse standing. Horses with broken legs cannot exercise and have to stand for six to eight weeks while the fracture heals.)

They asked me the cost. I could see money was not plentiful, so I brought the price way down. I also said that when I was in the area, I would stop by to check on the horse at no additional cost. That made the little girl and her mother feel better.

I splinted the leg and put a sling on the mare. I left medicine and instructions on how to care for the patient. Every time I stopped by to check, the horse was doing well.

Just before Christmas, it was time to take the sling and splint off. The mare had healed beautifully and could walk on the leg. I gave the little girl and her mother more instructions on the therapy the mare needed to recover after two months of not walking.

When I was putting my equipment back in my truck, the mother asked me to come in for coffee. My rule had always been not to go in a client's house when just a woman was there. But the little girl said, "Come in. I want to give you something."

The look in her eyes told me I could not refuse her request. It was a clean house, but pretty bare in the way of furniture. We visited while we drank coffee. I said I really needed to be on my way. The little girl replied, "Wait, I have something for you."

She came back with a sack of candy.

"I got this candy last night when we went to church," she said. "I want to pay you."

The next moment is still tough for me to think about. It always brings tears to my eyes.

Her mother told me, "That's the only Christmas present she has." They couldn't afford anything else.

You know, I can still see that little girl. There isn't a Christmas that goes by when I don't think of her. I wonder what happened to her.

When I performed that procedure on the horse, I knew the chances of the leg healing were not very good. But she healed anyway. And I believe the passenger in my truck had a lot to do with it.

Yes, God was my passenger. I talked to Him every day.

CHAPTER TWENTY-THREE

Horse Observations

After working with animals for many years, I have concluded that people and animals share certain characteristics.

For example, my wife would sometimes come home from a committee meeting and say she didn't like so-and-so because she was so bossy. And I would just laugh to myself and say, "Dominance."

Humans have a soul and can reason on a much larger scale than animals. However, some species of animals are smarter than others. In this chapter, I will share some observations I've made about horses over the years.

THE BOSS

I will start by just telling you a little story. Lester Ellerbush, who has passed away, was an old-time Belgian draft horse breeder. He had years of experience working with draft horses. Once, while I was visiting with him at his farm, he lifted up his shirt to show me a big bandage on his back.

"What happened there, Lester?"

"You see that old guy over there?" he asked as he pointed to a stall where an old stallion was kept. "He is about fifteen years old. I've never had any trouble with him in the many years I have owned him."

Lester continued talking. "The other day, the light bulb was burned out in his stall. I grabbed the ladder and a new light bulb and went in. The stallion was outside, but he could go in and out at his pleasure. I set the ladder, then climbed up a few steps to change the bulb. That old fool grabbed me by the back and tossed me into the corner. He struck me with his front feet and bit me wherever he could. I happened to have a hammer in my hand. I beat him across the nose and face and got away. If I hadn't had that hammer, he would have killed me.

"Doc, you know he and I had to reestablish *who was the chief around here*," he finished. "Because that stallion thought *he* was the boss."

The moral of the story? On some farms, the draft horse thinks he is the boss. When that happens, the horse needs to be retrained.

HOW DO THEY KNOW?

There is one thing I have often wondered about, but I've never found an answer for it.

At the farm where I kept my breeding stock, we kept the stallion in a box stall with a door, through which he could go out into the exercise pen. The pen had solid board walls about twelve feet high.

The farthest point in the pasture from the barn was about three quarters of a mile. If the mares and the foals were down in the pasture and we wanted to bring them home, we would take the saddle horse—a gelding—and ride down and bring them up to the yard.

The stud could not see the herd, nor could he smell them. Yet when the rider approached the mares with the gelding, the stud would throw an absolute fit. In his mind, another stallion was with his band of mares.

We ran this experiment a number of times. I could never figure out how that stallion knew that gelding was with the mares.

And it wasn't just on my farm. One time, I was on an Amish farm in Indiana where the breeder had two stallions in box stalls in a barn. Down the road, a half of mile from these stallions, he had another stallion in a barn. He sent his boy to get this other stallion and bring him to the homestead.

While we were waiting for the boy to come with the stallion, he remarked, "Watch these two stallions in the barn. When the boy comes out on the road with the younger stud, they will throw a fit."

And that is exactly what happened.

There was no way these stallions could see, hear, or know the boy was bringing another stallion home. It has always been a wonder to me that stallions can keep track of each other so well, and that they can sense a gelding and assume it is a stud.

Many horse people know about this amazing phenomenon, but everyone just shrugs their shoulders when I ask how it happens.

DOMINANCE

The stallion is always the dominant horse in a band of mares. This is especially true in wild horses. The stallion decides when the band goes to water or when to move. Foals, however, are not bothered by dominance in the first part of their lives.

Every band also has a dominant mare. Below the dominant mare, the remaining mares are ranked by submissiveness. They keep their placement in the rank. The most submissive mare will not find a place at the feed bunk unless there is plenty of room.

If a horse owner buys a new mare that happened to be the dominant mare in her herd, he will have trouble. The two dominant mares will fight it out. If a submissive mare is added to the herd, there will be just a little squeal and a kick or two. She will soon settle into her place.

When loading a team onto a trailer, it will go easier if you load the dominant animal first. For example, once I had a team I drove with a buggy. It was a gelding and a mare, and the gelding was the dominant one of the two. He had to be harnessed first, and when loading the team onto a trailer he had to be the first one on. The submissive mare refused to load first. The same was true for my two mules, Maude and Sarah. When I led Maude, Sarah would follow right behind without being tied.

Some people say my mules worked this way because of the way they were trained. There is some truth in that. But even when they weren't working, Maude was always first to the feed and first out the door. In general, the dominant animal will come to feed first, while the most submissive ones wait for the opportunity to come in. The submissive ones will only feed if the dominant one allows it.

When handling and treating these animals, a vet can use this dominance pattern to his advantage. If you lead the dominant animal, the rest will follow.

But, as the first story in this chapter demonstrates, horses need to be trained to recognize the owner as the ultimate boss. It takes work.

HORSES AND DEATH

I have often wondered in my practice what animals know about death. They must understand it to some degree. Otherwise, why would they fight so hard to stay alive? No one has ever answered that question for me. But I believe that if animals didn't know about death, they wouldn't struggle like they do. They would just lie down to die.

A horse will look directly at you when he is about to die. Many times in my work, I walked up to a horse that had been stricken. After looking at its eyes, I would say to the owner, "Step aside. He is going to drop dead."

Often, the horse dropped while we were standing there.

A MEAN PERCHERON

In my practice, I was called to castrate many of the horses that came out of the government's Adopt a Wild Horse program. If I could get the wild horse between a gate and a wall, I could get a tranquilizer into its vein. But many of those horses were a real handful.

One of these horses became quite famous. Two brothers in southern Iowa were in the horse-pulling business. They had bought a big, dapple-gray Percheron stallion that was about three years old. He was not only mean, but wise to the ways of man. The owners had called a number of veterinarians to get him castrated. They were all unsuccessful.

The brothers were positive that if they could get him trained in horse-pulling, the stallion would be worth quite a bit of money. Orville Pierce and I went down to the farm to see if we could get the job done. By his reputation, we knew this horse would bite, kick, and stomp out our lives if he was given the opportunity.

In order to handle him, we got the stallion into a cattle chute. We didn't want him in the stanchion at the end of the chute. (A horse fight in a stanchion is something terrible and can lead to the horse choking itself.) The stallion fought, trying to get out. I got my first injection into his vein after quite a few attempts. As the tranquilizer began to take effect, he calmed down, and I got the anesthetic into his vein. He was only supposed to be on his feet for a couple minutes after receiving these shots.

We opened the chute, the stallion jumped out, and ended up going down under a yard gate. We had to lift the gate off its hinges to get to him. It took all our strength to roll that big horse over to neuter him.

The owners trained the horse well. He was sold to some pullers in the state of Oregon. I heard through the grapevine that he became one of the top pulling horses in that part of the country.

RUNAWAY WITH A MANURE SPREADER

I had a team of drafts that we used to haul manure and do work around the farm. They were trained to work, but they were a pair that you had to watch. You didn't want to be asleep when you were driving them.

Bob Mouw and I had hauled quite a few loads of manure out to the field the previous day. We had two spreaders, each with a team. Mr. Mouw would load both spreaders—mine first, then his. We would spread at the same time.

We worked in the morning that way. I was just taking out my last load—the thirteenth load, for you superstitious folks. I spread the load on the field of cornstalks. I stopped the spreader to take it out of gear. As I bent over, something scared the team, and they took off at a trot—not a run. They turned sharply to the right. I was leaning in that direction and fell off.

I was being dragged through the cornstalks, between the wheels of the spreader. I was still holding onto the reins. When the team started trotting faster, I knew I had to let go.

So I did. The rear wheel ran over my hand and body. The horses then trotted back to where we had been loading the spreader.

Mr. Mouw came running when he saw the team of horses return with no driver. I was still conscious when the ambulance arrived. My whole left side was swollen, black and blue. The broken ribs were very painful.

We never did figure out what spooked the team. All the other loads had gone perfectly.

It just goes to show that when you work around animals, you never know what will happen. So it is important to be alert. If a horse gets frightened, he is going to invoke a flight pattern. In the wild, he will run away and then turn around, using his eyes, nose, and ears to figure out what scared him. That behavior is just part of the psychology of the horse.

Clearly, they still possess that trait today.

Draft mares enjoying a summer day.

A group of Belgian mares on our farm east of Orange City.

Photo courtesy of Dan, Theresa, and Ryan Mc Carty.

A man and his horse.

My horses enjoying time in the pasture.

Photo courtesy of Dan, Theresa, and Ryan McCarty.

CHAPTER TWENTY-FOUR

Draft Horse Journal, Horse Clinics, and Judging Fairs

When my veterinary career ended, I had no idea what God had planned for the rest of my life. After my unexpected teaching debut at a draft horse seminar (more on that later in this chapter), more clinic requests came in. My focus became draft horses and, subsequently, draft mules.

There was no way Mary and I could have known how this transition was going to impact our lives, the places we would travel, and the wonderful people we would meet.

Draft Horse Journal

In the early eighties, I began writing articles for *Draft Horse Journal*, a magazine based in Waverly, Iowa. The *Journal* was published four times a year. During the twenty-plus years I wrote for the magazine, I had one or two articles in each issue and covered a variety of subjects. Most of the time, I wrote informative articles on taking care of draft horses, though sometimes I just told a good story. The *Draft Horse Journal* eventually put many of my articles online.

I sometimes received responses in the mail after an issue of the magazine was published. My article on treating lockjaw was published more than once. Later, when people would call and tell me they had a horse with tetanus, I would refer them to the online posting of these articles.

MAURY TELLEEN

Maury Telleen was the founder and editor of *Draft Horse Journal*. He and his wife, Jeannine, became good friends of ours. Mr. Telleen was instrumental in encouraging me to judge horse shows and teach at clinics. I eventually taught clinics all around the country and on my farm. My wife often accompanied me. She enjoyed getting out and meeting draft horse clientele.

But that first clinic came as a bit of a surprise to me.

Mr. Telleen invited Mary Virginia and me to a horse event in Michigan. It worked with our schedule, so we decided to go. We drove to Waverly, where the Telleens lived, and rode the rest of the way together. The clinic was to be a forum on judging the soundness of a draft horse.

As we got close to the college in Michigan where the clinic was being held, the course of our conversation changed.

"Neumann, you are on the program today!" announced Mr. Telleen.

"I am?" I managed to stammer out.

"You *are* the program," he said. "We will have six horses for you to judge. You are to present an overview of their soundness."

If it had been possible to go home right then, I would have.

When we arrived at the livestock facilities at the college, Mr. Telleen left us while he made sure everything was ready. Soon, he came back to explain that only one horse was available for the class demonstration, but they were looking for more. He was highly distraught. He then asked if I could "B.S." these people for about forty-five minutes while they got more horses.

I couldn't let my friend down. So, I went in front of those gathered around the old, white draft horse and talked about its faults for a while.

That is how Maury Telleen—the son of a gun—did it to me.

Horse Clinics

That clinic was the beginning of a whole new chapter in my life. I started traveling, conducting clinics all over the country and in Canada.

CELEBRATING FIFTY YEARS OF MARRIAGE

For a number of years, I traveled to California each November to teach a four-day clinic with Fred Polinder, Jr., and his wife. I had met Mr. Polinder at a clinic in Michigan, where we were both instructors.

In California, we taught at two different fairgrounds. I covered judging the soundness and health of a draft horse and hitching problems you may encounter. Mrs. Polinder taught how to braid manes and tails for a show, while her husband showed students how to drive a single-horse to a six-horse hitch. It was a good school, organized by auctioneers Merlin and Marilyn Carlson. The classes coordinated with a Carlson auction and had an average size of twenty students.

Mary went along about half the time. Our fiftieth wedding anniversary was celebrated on November 5, during one of these clinics. They had a big party for us, the Carlsons, and the Polinders. (Our anniversaries were all around that time.) It was a total surprise to Mary and me. A number of students from previous years came. Even a college classmate of mine and his wife drove down from Washington state to wish us well. A large meal was served to everyone.

My poor wife couldn't get away from the horses, even on our anniversary. But she didn't complain. She was a trooper through it all!

HORSE CLINICS AT OUR FARM

Bob Mouw and I gave a number of four-day clinics called "All About the Draft Horse." Students came to my farm to learn about health and selecting a good, sound draft horse. They would then go to Mr. Mouw's farm, where he taught harnessing, hitching, and working the draft horse. He would take an unbroken horse and demonstrate how to train it.

A typical class was made up of four or five people, though we sometimes had eight or nine. At first, we only held the clinics four times a year. But as more people heard about them and wanted to come, we started holding them every other month.

We taught students from a wide variety of backgrounds. Some were farmers, others were draft horse breeders. They came from all across the United States, plus Columbia and Canada.

One of our students was a deep-sea diver. As he was leaving, he said he was going to send Mr. Mouw and me a present. When the package was delivered and opened, we found a parcel of live lobsters. The student had told us that when he was working, he was sometimes surrounded by lobsters…but it was illegal to take them!

Another student was a very wealthy gentleman from California who had just purchased a mare for $30,000 at a draft horse sale in Iowa. You can believe I sweated the whole time that horse was on my farm. I was so afraid something might happen to her.

IOWA'S COLD WINTERS

Our barn was heated, which made it possible to hold clinics in the winter. Several of these winter classes were made up of army personnel from the Caisson Platoon. One of these men had heard about our harsh Iowa winters, so he came prepared for the cold. He called a friend who had been stationed in Alaska and got a set of military-issue winter clothing.

```
                                    FEBRUARY 4, 1993

    THE DRAFT HORSE JOURNAL
    P.O. BOX 670
    WAVERLY, IOWA 50677
    ATTN: MAURICE TELLEEN

    DEAR MAURICE,

        I FEEL COMPELLED TO WRITE THIS LETTER, AFTER ARRIVING HOME FROM
    ORANGE CITY, IOWA.

        IF YOU RECALL, I WAS UNDECIDED ABOUT ATTENDING THE "WOODEN SHOE
    DRAFT HORSE SCHOOL" AND CALLED YOU TO ASK FOR SOME WELL NEEDED
    INFORMATION PERTAINING TO THE SCHOOL. AFTER SPEAKING WITH YOU, I
    PROCEEDED TO CALL MR. J. WILLIAM REED OF FREDRICKSTOWN, OHIO, WHO HAS
    HELPED ME MORE WITH MY HORSES AND NEEDED INFORMATION, AND ASKED HIS
    OPINION ABOUT THE SCHOOL. YOU AND BILL REED BOTH TOLD ME I COULDN'T
    GO WRONG BY ATTENDING. WELL YOU BOTH WERE ABSOLUTELY CORRECT.

        I CANNOT PUT INTO WORDS THE EDUCATIONAL REWARDS I RECEIVED, COUPLED
    WITH THE COMPLETE HANDS ON EXPERIENCE AFFORDED ME BY "DOC" NEUMANN. I
    STRONGLY RECOMMEND TO ANYONE WHO HASN'T OR HESITATES TO TAKE THIS
    COURSE, AND WHO IS INTERESTED IN BETTERING THEIR KNOWLEDGE OF
    HORSEMANSHIP, BOTH LIGHT AND DRAFT; YOU ARE MISSING THE OPPORTUNITY
    OF A LIFETIME.

        " DOC" HAS A TALENT OF BEING ABLE NOT ONLY TO TEACH BUT ALSO TO
    SHOW YOU EXACTLY WHAT HE IS TALKING ABOUT, LEAVING NO QUESTIONS,
    UNANSWERED. HIS VAST KNOWLEDGE OF HORSEMANSHIP AND VETERINARY
    MEDICINE COUPLED WITH HIS WHIT AND PERSONALITY IS A DEFINITE WINNING
    COMBINATION. "DOC" IS A GREAT ASSET TO THE DRAFT HORSE FIELD.

        "DOC'S" WIFE MARY DOES AND OUTSTANDING JOB WITH THE DIFFICULT TASK
    OF COOKING AND MAKING SURE EVERYBODY HAS ENOUGH TO EAT AS WELL AS
    KEEPING EVERYONE ON SCHEDULE. SHE SEEMS TO BE ALWAYS WAITING FOR
    "DOC" !!

        IN CLOSING I CANNOT STRONGLY ENOUGH, RECOMMEND THIS COURSE OF STUDY
    TO ANYONE WHO HAS ANY INTEREST IN HORSES AND WANTS TO BETTER
    "HIMSELF".
                            SINCERELY YOURS,

                            RICHARD "GABE" GABELMANN
```

We received many similar letters after hosting a draft horse clinic.

He was protected from the cold all right. Once he had it all on, he could hardly walk and had to lie down in the bobsled we used for class. With that great, big hood on, all you could see were his eyes.

"I am ready for your Iowa cold," he said.

THE CHEF

Having clinics at the farm did make a lot of extra work for Mary Virginia. Each day, she served a big dinner at noon in our house.

Mrs. Mouw would come over to help serve and clean up. She often bought the desserts.

At the time we were giving clinics, none of the restaurants in the area were open on Sunday. So Mary would also serve bacon, eggs, toast, pancakes, and plenty of coffee on those mornings.

THE MULES OF NEW ORLEANS

Jackson Square is a historic park in the French Quarter of New Orleans. Mule-drawn carriage rides are available for tourists who want to experience the historic sites of the city.

But at one time, the city was having difficulty finding drivers and inspectors for the carriages. There was also some controversy, because the city didn't have standardized procedures for handling the mules. Several organizations were concerned about how the mules were watered and when they were taken off the line because of the heat.

The city of New Orleans called me. Three private enterprises owned the mules and carriages and were responsible for their operation. But the businesses were subject to regulations put out by the cab department of New Orleans, which licensed them to be on the street. The city wanted to develop a program that would keep everyone happy and allow these popular carriage rides to continue.

I was asked to go down there, look their operations over, and figure out what we could do to improve the situation. If I found anything that needed fixing, they would look into it.

The man in charge had worked in the water division of the city engineering department. I taught him and his team about inspecting the mules and preventing health problems with proper care and handling.

After that, I developed a program for inspecting the carriages. It was important for someone to be trained to make sure they were safe to hit the streets and transport people on their sightseeing tours.

The mule inspectors had to supervise watering and determine when the animals had to be taken off duty because of the heat. Each mule usually worked an eight-hour shift. They were to come into Jackson Square regularly for water. A thermometer was hung there, and when it reached a certain temperature the mules had to be retired. There were always representatives from animal welfare groups watching to make sure the city followed the set standards.

We brought in watering troughs for the mules that were filled using hydrants. But we had problems with people turning the water on and wasting it, so we had to put locks on the hydrants. People also began urinating in the troughs, which contaminated the water and necessitated extra cleaning. Instead of relying on the troughs, drivers began carrying a bucket to water the mules. That worked for a while, until someone complained that each mule should have its own bucket and with its name on it. So, in the end each mule was given an individualized bucket.

Once the standards for the program were set, the city advertised that it needed mule inspectors. My next job was training the applicants. We held a class, and the applicants with the highest scores were hired. The job included benefits, making it a highly desirable position. Once they had enough trained inspectors, my role in the project would be complete.

I will never forget this one woman who took the class. She was vastly overweight and came with a big bottle of Coke and a sack of potato chips. I was teaching them how to pick up a mule's foot to check if the shoe needed replacing. She was eating her chips and drinking her pop. I asked her to pick the mule's foot up. In her Southern drawl, she said to me, "I won't touch no mule."

We were told not to flunk anyone, but I could give them a low grade. Each class had about ten to twelve students, out of which the top few were certified to become inspectors. Practically none of the students had prior experience with mules. The carriage inspectors, on the other hand, were fairly easy to teach once I got the program set up.

In addition to training inspectors, I also took a look at the mules. First, I went to the mule barns. The three businesses that owned the mules already had certain rules and regulations in place. As stated earlier, a mule worked eight hours out of twenty-four. They would do that for so many months, then would have two or three months off in a pasture.

All these mules had to be identified. Many were black, and to the casual observer they all looked the same. A serial number was tattooed on their lips. Records were kept on each mule, though the owners had to be talked into keeping these records current.

A mule is a *different* kind of animal. They become used to certain people. Sometimes, a mule will only tolerate one driver, which is something people have to keep in mind when working with them.

Exhibit A. One of the mule owners was an elderly man who kept his stables down by the housing projects. I went to see his mules with a city employee, who told me to ask the owner about the mule that caught the fugitive.

So I asked the man, "Say, I hear you had something to do with a police chase?"

"Yes, sir," he answered. "That is a good story."

Down in New Orleans, their sheds are shaped like a horseshoe. Work is done in the center courtyard.

"One morning, I was out feeding the mules," the man said. "I heard a commotion on the other side of the shed. I saw a man run along the roof and jump to the ground. Then he jumped over a fence into a pen containing this one mule.

"The police had been chasing this man. They saw him come my way, so they asked me if I had seen a running man," he continued. "I told them I hadn't seen anyone."

After the police left, the mule owner went to the shed the fugitive had entered. He found him in a stall, cornered by the mule.

"Let me out," the fugitive had said. "This mule is not letting me go anywhere."

"I can't. The only person that can handle that mule is his driver," the owner explained. "He won't be here until this afternoon. I can't even go in there—that stall belongs to the mule, and he isn't going to share it."

When the mule's driver came, the fugitive was released from mule custody into police custody.

My time in New Orleans was fun. We were there in the summertime and trained some good inspectors. I continued to make trips there throughout the eighties and nineties. Most of the time, Mary Virginia went with me.

HAWAIIAN PARADISE

At one time, a hotel chain built a new resort on the Hawaiian island of Kauai, complete with top-of-the-line golf courses. It was located right by the dock where people came off cruise ships. It also had a huge swimming pool right next to the ocean. The place was beautiful, and it had cost a great deal of money to build.

If you wanted to go from the main hotel to The Cliff, the resort's special dining area, a boat or carriage would take you. The complex was designed to resemble Venice, with canals connecting places of interest. Draft horses hitched to carriages also transported visitors on pink coral paths.

Beautiful stables housed sixty draft horses brought in from the mainland. There were outdoor runs for the horses, and their fancy carriages were built in Canada. Each vehicle was handmade and double-seated.

They were having problems with the draft horses and carriages. They hardly had enough horses to handle the carriages, because some horses were lame or had sores on their shoulders. The people from California who had sold the horses to the hotel were brought to the island to get things back on track. A team of veterinarians from the University of California, Davis, also came to fix the problem. But they were unsuccessful, and the owners of the resort were getting desperate.

They called me in 2001. I said I would go if my wife could also come. They treated us like royalty. We were welcomed with leis, and a limousine picked us up at the airport.

The state room they provided for us was absolutely out of this world. On one wall was a cabinet full of alcoholic and non-alcoholic drinks. Someone put flowers on the pillows every night. If there was anything we wanted or needed, all we had to do was call and it would be ours. It was really something for two clodhoppers from Iowa!

On the first morning, when we went down for breakfast, the waitress and chefs introduced themselves to us.

"We love our horses," they said. "You are the person who came to save them, aren't you?"

"I will do the best I can," I reassured them.

The same man who had picked us up from the airport brought me to the main office. The general manager was seated behind his desk. Some other men were also standing in the room.

When the general manager looked at me, I was introduced as an equine specialist. He stared at me with eyes as cold as two icebergs. He looked like a rattlesnake ready to strike.

"I am sick and tired of you experts," he said.

I looked back at him.

"I didn't say I was an expert. I am a veterinarian," I replied. "I will look at your animals, and if I can't fix the problem, I will tell you."

"Follow me," he said.

We went to his limousine and drove to the office building near the stables. He told the foreman to get everyone into the meeting room. A quiet-looking crew came in.

He introduced me as a veterinarian who was going to look at the horses and try to straighten out the problem.

"You do what Dr. Neumann orders exactly," he instructed. "I am going to Chicago for a week to ten days. I expect things to be better when I get back."

He exited, leaving me alone with these frightened employees.

"I am not going to fire anyone," I reassured them. "We will find out what is wrong."

Those words changed their demeanor completely.

We got busy examining the horses and learning their histories. We discovered that the collar sores came from ill-fitting collars. We treated them with the proper medications, and new collars were purchased. The harnesses were not fitted correctly either, but that was easily changed.

I also discovered that the pink coral was sharp, and it would fly up under the horses' collars and irritate the sores. I told the team they needed to come up with a way to prevent that from happening.

The carriages were poorly designed for the horses' line of draft. I showed the blacksmiths and carpenters how the carriages needed to be rebuilt. The horses' diet also needed changing. Specifically, they needed more roughage. We also set regular hours for the horses: eight hours to work, then at least eight hours of rest. We made sure each horse was offered enough water. To satisfy some watchers, each horse had to have its own bucket with its name on it.

We got this all done in the ten-day period. All the horses were back on the line but one, which had some terrible sores that took longer to heal.

We went home the same day the general manager got back from Chicago. I didn't even talk to him.

The hotel was a fabulous place to visit. I got up early in the morning and worked late into the night. Two workers asked why I didn't play golf like all the other horse doctors.

"Two reasons. Number one, I don't play golf," I said. "Reason number two. I was hired to do a job, and I can't do the job if I am golfing."

Some of the staff also opened the liquor cupboards. "You haven't touched any of this," they remarked.

"I came here to work, not drink," I answered. I didn't want to go to work with liquor on my breath.

Mary, on the other hand, enjoyed a real vacation. She loved to swim. (She had been on a swimming team in Ames.) She could swim there at the beach or walk right out of the ocean to a beautiful pool.

Out of gratitude, the employees treated us to a night at The Cliff. When Mary and I saw that the price of the first course was $45, we were shocked. The staff then wheeled a really nice piano out and played whatever music we requested.

After we arrived at home, the manager sent us a letter. He invited us to come back. Everything was rolling along just perfectly, and they were planning a special party for us. They sent us airplane tickets, and we went just before Christmas.

At the party, the manager told my wife, "You know, we should have had Doc Neumann here from the start. Those other people didn't do us a bit of good. He is the best veterinarian we have seen."

By the time of the party, a young veterinarian was on staff to care for the horses.

A few years later, a hurricane destroyed the resort. It was never rebuilt.

BOARD OF DIRECTORS

One day the phone rang. It was the Belgian Draft Horse Corporation of America. Unknown to me, my name had been placed on the Board of Directors ballot. I was chosen. I served three consecutive three-year terms in the 1990s.

Judging Fairs

I was asked to judge draft horse shows at fairs scattered across the United States. Kansas, Maryland, North Carolina, and Virginia were a few of the state fairs I judged. When someone would call to ask me to judge a show, I would say, "Yes…but my wife comes, too."

"Absolutely," they would always say. "She is also welcome."

One thing I learned as a judge is that not everyone will be satisfied with your results. I always told anyone who complained that it was just my opinion; someone else could certainly have a different one. I always tried to be honest and do the best I could, and complaints only happened once in a great while. Overall, I enjoyed judging horse shows because I was able to see good stock and meet many wonderful people.

A WET FAIR

One time, I was judging at one of the oldest horse shows in the country. It was a show with many classes and was held outdoors in front of a grandstand. It had been raining all day, but it began to pour around the time of the show.

I said to the fair officials, "Surely you aren't going to have the horse show today!"

Despite the muddy track conditions and rainstorm, the horse show went on as planned. Every time the horses came by, I was splashed with mud. The horses, the wagons, and their owners were absolutely covered with muck. It was impossible to do a good job.

DRIVING CLASSES IN VIRGINIA

At the Virginia State Fair, I judged the hitch classes, where contestants entered both mules and draft horses. Belgian, Clydesdale, Percheron, mule—they were all represented.

Mary and our daughter, Penny Jo, were at the gate where exhibitors entered the show arena. There was one elderly, tobacco-chewing exhibitor who was driving six good mules hitched to a decrepit tobacco wagon.

According to the rules of the fair, I was to judge the draft horses and mules solely for their driving ability. This man with his old tobacco wagon and mules was entered in the six up draft horse and mule driving class. He was competing against real fancy wagons and draft horses with immaculate harnesses.

During the competition, the mules outdid the draft horses in the maneuvers. So, he received first place. Second place went to a young man with Belgians.

After the show, Mary and Penny Jo told me they could hear the old man muttering before he went in the gate.

"Heck, no use going in there. No Yankee is going to put me in first place."

Because I was interested in how he trained those mules so well, I visited with him. Despite his appearances, the man was a wealthy landowner who had turned most of his farmland over to his sons. He had retained eighty acres so he could continue to farm with his mules. It was no wonder they did so well. He worked with them every day.

One can't always judge a book by its cover.

PRISON HORSES

A friend from Alabama came to watch me judge the Mississippi State Fair. After the show was over, he told me the hitch that had won most the driving classes was from a prison farm in Alabama. They used horses at the prison, and prisoners were showing the hitch. Their horses were in good shape, and the prisoners knew how to show and handle them.

UNDER SADDLE

In the past few years, various shows have included a draft horse under saddle class. In this class, the draft horse is actually ridden, and the rider and horse are both judged.

I was judging this class at a state fair. Before the contestants entered the arena, the ringmaster told me he had some instructions for me.

"Dr. Neumann, we have a favor to ask you," he said.

"What's that?" I asked.

"We prefer that you do not ask the contestants to dismount," he replied. "Last year, we held this particular class for the first time. All the contestants were heavyset women. When the judge told them to dismount, they did…but they were not able to get back on the horse. They had to have all kinds of help, and the crowd roared with laughter."

I did not ask the contestants to dismount.

Me teaching about draft horses at one of my many clinics.

Fred and Glenda Polinder, Mary and me, and Marilyn and Merlin Carlson celebrating our fiftieth wedding anniversaries in California.

Fred Polinder, myself, and Merlin Carlson enjoyed a strong friendship and mutual love for draft horses.

A Percheron draft horse at one my classes.

Teaching classes kept me busy.

Me giving a closeup view of a horse's hoof.

At our classes, Bob Mouw taught trainning, hitching, and working the draft horse.

Bob Mouw with a student.

I have judged at many shows over the years.

CHAPTER TWENTY-FIVE

"Mary, We Are Going to Australia!"

I have some professional connections to the Budweiser Farm. In the 1990s, their Clydesdale man called me to ask if I wanted to judge the Royal Easter Fair in Sydney, Australia. Fair organizers had asked him to be a judge, but his health prevented his going. So, he told them he would help find someone to go in his place. He thought of me, which I felt was quite an honor.

"Sure, I will go," I said. "But I could use a little training in judging Clydesdales."

"We'll teach you," he replied.

So I went to his home in Illinois, and he taught me a number of things specific to the Clydesdale breed.

THE ROYAL EASTER FAIR

In the 1990s, Clydesdales made up ninety-nine percent of Australian draft horses. They are revered by Australians, similar to how Americans view the bald eagle.

Mary Virginia and I went to Australia. The Royal Easter Fair is by far the biggest agricultural fair and the greatest show I have ever seen. Truly, I have never seen so much livestock at any fair or show anywhere else in the world.

Most of the livestock is shown outside on a racetrack. They run horse races around the track, while the interior is divided into four quarters—one ring of livestock in each quarter. The open-air stadium surrounding the racetrack provides seating for spectators.

Judging draft horses in Australia was remarkably different than judging them in the States. The principal horse was the Clydesdale. Some of the classes had many entries, and eliminating a number of these animals would have been time consuming if it were done like the average show in the States.

I had the horses in the class I was judging walk or trot in a circle at my command. As the horses rotated around the horse stewards and myself, I picked out the ones I could see were in the top percentage of their class. The stewards moved the selected horses to another place for further judging. After that initial elimination, I could judge the selected horses the same as we do in the United States. This system worked very well.

I arrived a few days ahead of my scheduled events, so I could learn the ropes and watch the quarter horses being judged. The gentleman in charge of judging had been Supreme Commander of the Australian forces in the Pacific during WWII. It still makes me chuckle to think of what he said when I went out to judge my first class. He notified me that I could take as much time as I needed for any class. But then he said:

"You see that big hand on the clock over there? We expect you to be done by noon."

There really *was* a time limit, which I tried to adhere to. It was rather humorous when you think about it, though. Take as long as you want...but we expect you to be done at noon.

Despite the few differences I've noted, the classes and standards for judging were similar to those in the States. No matter where you are in the world, there are certain characteristics that make up a good, sound horse representative of its breed.

The Royal Easter Fair.
Photo courtesy of the Royal Agricultural Society of New South Wales Heritage Centre.

TIME PERIOD CLASS

There was one class, however, that I had never judged before: the time period class. Horses were hitched to vehicles from the era the entries were representing. Dress, vehicles, and harnesses all matched a specific point in history.

I gave first place to a fantastic hearse. The horses were all black, as were the harnesses. As with all the entries, I tried to trap the competitors. But I didn't get the job done.

They actually had a *dead* man inside that hearse—at least he really appeared to be deceased. He didn't bat an eye and was very white. I could hardly tell if he was breathing.

The minister up on the hearse had the Bible open.

"Sir, what verse are you reading?" I asked.

He quoted a verse from memory. I checked the Bible, and it was open to that verse.

All the entries were done in extremely good detail, but this one went above and beyond. It was a fun class to judge!

OUT OF THE BUSH

Judging the draft horses took five days, though there were some days we only worked half a day.

I enjoyed judging these Clydesdales. I took every opportunity to speak to the contestants showing the horses. One stalwart young man exhibiting a two-year-old Clyde filly took fourth in his class. As he received his ribbon and I fastened it in place around the neck of the mare, I said, "You have a real good mare. But it looks like you just shod her. If you had just trimmed those feet a little before shoeing her, you would have done better in the show."

"Sir, I am tickled to death," he replied. "I just got her out of the bush five days ago."

The grand champion was a Clydesdale mare. I found out later she had been the grand champion two years before. So I figured I must have done a decent job of judging. (I heard no complaints, anyway.)

I think the rule was if an animal was a grand champion it could not be shown for two years, thus giving others a chance to win. I remember the winner was an excellent animal. She had one very small blemish on her right front leg, but overall she was sound as a dollar.

HAT AND SUIT

One thing I learned very quickly was that judges needed to wear a hat in the ring. That sun was so intense that after the first day one of the Australians with us said, "Come on, Doc. We are going to buy you a hat that will protect your face." So I ended up wearing a real, broad-brim Australian hat. Some of those hats had a five-inch brim. Even the women wore hats.

Besides the hat, I was expected to wear a suit while judging. Mary and I went to the fairground the day after our arrival in Sydney to report to the secretary of the fair, who I had been corresponding with. After welcoming us, she said, "Dr. Neumann, I know you don't know this, but you must wear a suit, tie, and hat any time you are on the fairgrounds."

I knew I would be wearing a suit when I was judging, but I didn't expect to wear one on my leisure time!

PICK UP THE FOOT

The Australians paid attention to my judging. After the first class, the man in charge—the retired Supreme Commander—came and spoke to me.

"Dr. Neumann," he said. "In regard to your examination of the front foot of the horse, you need to pick up the foot to see that it is in a normal position when shod."

Sometimes, a draft horse's foot may turn to the left or the right. To cover this flaw, the foot may be trimmed to appear normal.

"No, sir. I can tell without picking the foot up," I said. "I will show you how with the next class."

As I was judging a horse, I showed him I could run my finger on the hoof head and determine the exact middle of the foot without picking it up.

"By jolly," he said in his Australian accent. "I learned something new today."

We stayed on after the Royal Easter Fair to tour the country with different Clydesdale breeders. I also judged a few smaller shows. We stayed with families right on their farms.

MELBOURNE

Our second trip to Australia occurred at the same time the Clydesdale Association had arranged a trip there. We didn't actually travel with them, but we tagged along.

When I judged at the Royal Easter Fair, the breeders were always talking about the big Clydesdale show in Melbourne. We got to see that show on our second trip. I was asked to judge some classes, which I thought was very nice. It rained the day I judged. The show was held outside, but the officials had a tent we could go into to dry off between classes.

I didn't have a raincoat, so I was introduced to the Australian oilskin. When the show was over, one of the Australians in our party took me to a clothing store, and I bought an oilskin of my own that still serves me well today.

Mary Virginia had packed a plastic raincoat for herself, just in case.

IN THE COUNTRY

We also gave a number of clinics on our second trip. One was at a brewery in Sydney that had a hitch very similar to the Budweiser Clydesdale eight-horse hitch. I also gave a clinic to a large number of people at a horseshoe factory. Again, we went out into the country, where our hosts showed us a number of interesting things. For example, we visited a big sheep ranch, where we watched sheep being sheared.

One family invited us to a political rally that was going to be held on a neighboring farm. Quite a number of people congregated for this rally. The family we were staying with brought a team and wagon to the event. I helped give rides to the children while the others talked politics. Everyone enjoyed that night. There was a big picnic and a demonstration of shearing sheep with an old-fashioned manual hand clipper. The wool was baled using a wool press—the old-school way of doing things.

THE BROWN SNAKE

One thing I saw in Australia that really impressed me was the brown snake. It is my understanding that this is one of the five deadliest snakes in the world.

We were traveling on a seldom-used road after leaving a sheep shearing. Mr. Watson, the Australian friend of ours who was driving, suddenly stopped the car.

"See that big snake lying across the road?" he asked. "We don't mess with him."

"Can I get out and take a picture?" I asked.

"You can get out, but don't go down the road," he advised. "Take the picture from right here."

When I took the picture, the brown snake moved.

"Get right back in here," Mr. Watson ordered me.

Later, my wife and I commented on how chickens were always running loose on Australian farms.

"How come you have your chickens running loose?" we asked.

"They keep the brown snakes away," we were told.

I would have kept them out, too.

AN INVITATION TO THE BRITISH GOVERNOR'S HOUSE

When I was judging at the Royal Easter Fair, we were invited to the British governor's residence for dinner, along with other judges and fair officials.

At a second dinner, where the president of Australia and his wife were present, they placed us at the head table. I sat next to the president, and my wife sat next to his wife. Just think: Mary Virginia and I sitting with all those dignitaries!

The meal was served in courses. They had so many pieces of silverware that I had to watch others to know which one to use.

Every night of the Royal Easter Fair, they put on a show in the arena. On one of these nights, we were asked to sit in the president's box at the fairgrounds. All the livestock was paraded out into the huge show ring where the competitions had taken place. It was dark, and the people leading the livestock carried lights. It was absolutely stunning.

Before the livestock parade, there was a parade of bands. The English Mounted Band performed on horseback, right before the president's box. They were well received. We couldn't have had a better seat.

The United States Marine Band had been performing in Hawaii, after which they flew to Australia to participate in this show. They came on the field playing "Waltzing Matilda." I swelled with pride for the United States when I heard the resulting cheers and applause from the Australian crowd.

There was also a show of skill for herding livestock. I was just astonished at the way the Australians could handle livestock, as well as their excellent horse-riding skills. They didn't use ropes or lariats, like our Western cowboys do. They used stock whips—what we used to call "black snakes." They rode horseback, driving all their cattle individually or in groups with their whips. The drover never touched an animal with his stock whip.

Here's a little story that proves how good they were with their whips. One time, an Australian man asked me if I wanted an apple, as we were standing near an apple tree. He was carrying his stock whip. He took the stock whip and snapped an apple off the tree for me.

To judge draft horses at the famed Royal Easter Fair was indeed an honor. It was my privilege to judge both this show and the Melbourne draft horse show. To date, I am the only living American to have done so.

This is the caption that appeared in the newspaper The Land, *New South Wales, Australia: "Best Shire exhibit at RES was Stallion, Wyee Anthony, owned by W. Lambert of Waverley and led by Trevor Philip, and Judge Dr. John Neumann, Orange City, Iowa, USA."*

Photo courtesy of the Royal Agricultural Society of New South Wales Heritage Centre.

CHAPTER TWENTY-SIX

An Invitation to Colombia

It was the beginning of a new century when I first flew into Bogotá, the capital of Colombia. I was traveling with two other men—Maury Telleen, the owner and editor of *Draft Horse Journal*, and Ralph House, a board member of the Draft Horse Association. Mrs. Telleen and Mary Virginia were also with us.

Colombia was having its first national draft horse show. Mr. House and Mr. Telleen did most of the judging. The presentation of horses in the various classes lacked finesse. It was a learning experience for everyone involved.

This trip was also the beginning of the stud book for the *Asociación Colombiana de Criadores de Tiro Pesado* (ATP), or the Colombian Draft Horse Association. Our job was to put horses into the book. We travelled to farms and ranches, looking at mares to determine if they should go into the Belgian or Percheron book; then, by breeding them with purebred stock, the Colombians could register the offspring.

In 2000, horsepower was popular on farms in Colombia. They had many good draft horses of Percheron stock descended from horses brought from Argentina.

Two years after the first trip, we went back to again judge the national show, which was an honor.

COLOMBIAN FARMS

Our trips to Colombia weren't all work. I liked the Colombian people, and they were very good to us. We were able to see many old ranches that dated back to the time the Spaniards came to Colombia.

The architecture was interesting. Often, the stables were connected right to the living quarters. You passed through a veranda to go from room to room in the house. Even the food was carried into the dining room through the veranda. The kitchen had old-school baking ovens.

Many times, the employees at the ranches could not speak English, but they wanted to communicate with us in the worst way. And we did communicate, by hook and by crook.

By our standards, the working people on these farms were poor. At one farm, the hostess, who was the wife of the farm manager, wanted to serve us coffee. There were eight of us in the party, but she only had four cups. So she served four of us, thoroughly washed the cups, and served the other four. We had a lot of fun that day.

Our days usually began with breakfast at the hotel and lunch out in the country. The meat served was usually beef or chicken. The evening meal was sometimes at the home we were visiting and sometimes at the hotel. One time, we stayed at an inn in the room where the president of Colombia had once slept. It was very plush!

We had been warned not to go out on our own. It was obvious we were foreigners, which put us at risk for kidnapping. We would stay in the hotel lobby until our host came in to get us. While waiting, we would drink really good coffee served by girls in their native costumes.

The first time we were in Colombia, we went into the countryside every day to observe horses for the registry book. The second time, we did not travel into the rural areas as much. Our hosts didn't trust it, as there was trouble with people who were fighting the government.

We went down a third time to again judge the national show. On my second and third trips, I was the only judge. On our last trip, horses were still being used on the farms. It was a wonderful climate for dairy stock. You didn't have to put up hay, as livestock could graze year-round.

BOGOTÁ

Bogotá is surrounded by a ring of mountains, so it looks like it sits in the flat bottom of a giant bowl. It is located on the Andean Plateau. The climate doesn't vary much more than a degree or two. Flowers are the main industry. At one time, ninety-nine percent of America's roses came from Bogotá. When we flew in, we thought we saw lakes below, but they were actually huge plastic greenhouses.

The other main industry is dairy. The countryside is full of Holstein cows. When we were there, they had portable milking parlors, most of which were pulled by horses. They didn't have many tractors. The dairymen would pull the milking parlor right into the pasture. The cows would come, and they were milked out in the open. The milk was put in big tanks on a horse-drawn wagon, which then travelled a few miles to a gathering place, where it was loaded on refrigerated trucks.

I will never forget the sight of those pastures. One morning, we were on the edge of the plains, where the mountains rose up steep and rugged. About a hundred mules came out of the mountains, each carrying two cans of milk to be loaded onto the truck.

The Colombians who drove us around all owned draft horses and farms. Many of these farmers lived in the city and had managers who hired laborers to work on the farm. A number of these laborers lived on the farms where they were employed. The farms were beautiful places, with beautiful homes.

PROVING HEIFERS

On our second trip, Mary and I went to a ranch outside Bogotá that raised fighting bulls. The bulls were big and black, with nasty temperaments and menacing-looking horns.

On this day, they were testing heifers. The bull fighting ring on the ranch was surrounded by a stone wall. A heifer would be brought in. Then a man on a horse—which wore a protective, mattress-like covering—would strike the heifer's top shoulder with a two-foot, spear-like dart to enrage her.

The heifer would get angry and attack the horse. She was to be stuck with the dart three times, and each time she had to attack the horse and rider. If she failed, she went to slaughter. After that round of testing, a bull fighter would go in with his cape. He also had to be attacked three times. If the heifer displayed anger, she was kept to breed and raise fighting bulls.

We were sitting up on top of the wide stone wall. It had been a fun day, watching the bull testing going on below. I had a couple shots of *aqua dante*, a Colombian alcoholic drink. Somewhere, I heard someone calling my name. I could pick out, "Dr. Neumann, Dr. Neumann." The rest I could not understand because it was in Spanish. I asked my host what it was they wanted.

"They want you down there," he answered.

I went down to the gate by the arena.

"This heifer is going to fight, and you are going out there," the gatekeeper informed me.

Well, I didn't want to be a coward before all these people. The *aqua dante* had also bolstered my spirit, which probably had something to do with me agreeing.

Down in the arena, those heifers look even bigger.

I wasn't alone. The matador was also there. "We will hold this cape," he instructed me. "She will charge the cape. Then you must turn around because she will charge us again."

I just nodded my head in agreement.

"If the cape falls on the ground," he warned. "She may just take us."

We did this a couple of times together, then he gave me the cape.

"Goodbye," he said, before waving and escaping through an opening.

There I was, out in the arena with that angry heifer. I held the cape out. *Zippo*, she went right through it. I quickly turned around to hold the cape for four or five more passes. She was nasty enough that she was saved to raise bulls.

I was glad to be out of that pen in one piece. That heifer had a wicked set of horns, and she was looking to do me great bodily harm. Everyone was laughing and cheering me on, but I paid attention to the heifer.

My wife captured this episode on tape.

THANKFUL FOR A SUIT COAT

On our second trip to Bogotá, it was just the Telleens, Mary, and me. We were invited to hold a clinic at a Clydesdale breeder's farm. It was owned by a woman who was quite wealthy. When we got there in the morning, she came to me with a request.

"I have a mare that is foaling," she said. "She has been at it for some time and is having trouble."

Her three vets were not having success in helping the mare. After taking my suit coat, shirt, and tie off, I examined the mare and unborn foal. The legs of the foal needed to be straightened out. Once that was done, the foal was born in a very short time. The foal was dead, but I was told later that the mare made a full recovery.

In the process of delivering the foal, I ripped the seam in the seat of my khaki slacks. Fortunately, only the Telleens and Mary saw it.

I cleaned up and dressed again, but I couldn't mend my slacks. For the rest of the day, I had to be extra careful how I moved.

Maury Telleen videoed our clinic, including the delivery of the foal. The camera caught the sound of my slacks ripping, which the Telleens and Mary kidded me about. We had many good laughs over those torn pants.

But it was no laughing matter for the veterinarians who could not deliver the foal. The Clydesdale owner fired all three from her employment. I felt sorry about that.

On our third trip, the clinics were held on a farm at the edge of Bogotá, as the unrest in the countryside made it too dangerous for us to leave the city. We never went back to that beautiful country, but some Colombians came to the clinics at our farm in Iowa.

MARY SHOPS

The women always treated Mary Virginia well and planned things for her to do. Naturally, they went shopping. She purchased emerald stones. (In Australia, she had also bought emeralds from a gemologist in Sydney. Mary got stones for everyone on our world travels!)

DRUG TRADE

We toured a greenhouse that had acres and acres of flowers inside. It also had problems with the drug trade.

The florist told us it was a constant battle to keep drugs out of the flower shipments. The truck would be loaded free of drugs, but by the time it got to the airport there would be cocaine or other illegal substances hidden with the flowers. This would ruin the shipment.

At the airport, after we had been cleared by security, we sat in a little room to wait for our flight number to be called. We watched the men load the plane from the window. Sometimes, they would throw a bag off.

Soldiers walked through the area with drug-sniffing dogs. These men were wearing cavalry uniforms, like we'd had at one time in the United States.

I asked one soldier, "How come you are wearing cavalry clothing?"

He laughed. "We are the dog outfit, but there isn't money for uniforms. A long time ago, we received these uniforms from the United States. Now we are wearing them out."

I told him they looked sharp and that this was a good use for the uniforms.

A TENSE SITUATION

The only time Mary and I were a little bit nervous about being in a foreign country was in Bogotá. One night, some of the people with us asked if we wanted to drive by the presidential palace. They said it was pretty at night.

Mary and I sat in the back seat of the car. When riding down the street, we were stopped by an army patrol. No one in the patrol could speak English. Our guides were the translators.

The men looked under the car, inside the car, at the engine—all the time holding automatic weapons,

I said to Mary, "I hope these people we are with are honest."

Soon an army officer who could speak English arrived.

"Where are your passports?" he asked.

"We left them in the hotel, so we wouldn't lose them," we answered.

"Which hotel?"

Our passports were locked in a safe at the hotel. We had been instructed to leave them there, so they wouldn't be stolen. We were okay, but for a few minutes it was tense.

THE COLOMBIANS VISIT THE UNITED STATES

After the first time we went down to Bogotá, a group of Colombians came up to purchase draft horses and tour the Amish country in Ohio and Indiana.

Mary Virginia and I, along with Mr. and Mrs. Telleen, rode a tour bus with them for a week. They purchased quite a few draft horses. The Colombian women were interested in the horses, but they were *more* interested in shopping at the malls.

We parted in Chicago. They flew back to Columbia, and we drove back to Iowa.

A draft horse owner demonstrating his driving skills at his private ranch.

The courtyard of a hotel we stayed at in Colombia.

Milking cows, Colombia-style.

A picture of one the classes I taught in Colombia.

A group of Colombians I taught.

Shaking hands with the French Minister of Agriculture at a draft horse show in Colombia.

The red tie was a gift from the Minister of Agriculture.

CHAPTER TWENTY-SEVEN

His Mules, His Horses, His Antiques

A man needs his hobbies, and I am no exception. Hunting was something I always enjoyed doing—especially elk hunting, since it allowed me to indulge in my interest in mules.

My interest in the Civil War, on the other hand, was an offshoot of my passion for horses. Prior to the Civil War Centennial, I asked Bob Bonnecroy, Abe Schiebout, and Al Hancock, who was later replaced by Gerrit Hulstein, to join me in forming a cavalry unit. We outfitted our horses and ourselves in authentic gear. Our first show was at a parade in Armour, South Dakota. After that, I was hooked on antiques.

HUNTING

John Siemans, a college classmate and friend of mine, lived near Jackson Hole, Wyoming. I went to visit him in the fall of 1958. He talked me into getting a deer license.

Dr. Siemans intended to take me out hunting, but he got a call to vaccinate cattle. He talked his friend, Oral Wheeler, into taking me hunting instead. Mr. Wheeler was a professional outfitter; he took hunters, primarily elk and deer hunters, out to a camp in the mountains in the Jackson Hole area.

On that first hunting trip, I shot a near-record-book mule deer buck. Hunting elk and deer was now in my blood.

For many years, Mr. Wheeler and I hunted together. Sometimes, Mary Virginia would come along. When she did, she stayed at the ranch with Mr. Wheeler's wife.

THE MULES

Over the course of my hunting career, I became the owner of four good pack mules. The black mules, Jake and Joe, stayed at the ranch, where they were used when I went elk hunting. Maude and Sarah were big mules, weighing 1,200 pounds each. Jake and Joe were smaller, weighing about 1,000 pounds each.

The average mule is smarter than the average horse, but they do have to be handled a bit differently. A good example: You have never heard of mules making a cavalry charge. A mule does not want to be injured, so it reasons, "Boss, you may want to go out there and get shot…but I'm not going."

Another example: You take a mule and a horse down a trail and come to a bog. The horse will plunge right in and get stuck. Not the mule. It will stop and refuse to go any farther unless you find a way around it.

Generally, a mule will not overeat, but a horse will and pay for it by foundering.

One time, I didn't get the cinch tight enough on Jake. When I was unharnessing him, I noticed he had a little sore on his chest, right behind his left front leg. As he was eating, I went to get medicine to put on the cinch sore. I squirted some of the medicine on it. When Jake finished eating, I turned him loose.

The next day, as Jake was eating his morning grain, I examined the sore and decided to treat it again. As I held the bottle in position to give the wound a squirt, Jake kicked the medicine right out of my hand…without touching my fingers or even taking his nose out of the feed box. I decided Jake didn't need any more treatment.

Maude and Sarah were good pack mules. I just had to lead Maude, and Sarah would follow. She never had to be tied, because where Maude was Sarah would always be. Maude would not follow Sarah, though. She always had to be first.

On one trip, I shot my elk on the second day and brought it into camp. I had planned to stay in the hunting camp the next day, but I went with Mr. Wheeler when he asked if I would accompany him and his party of hunters to bring in a big elk they had shot. They would help load the elk on my mules, and I would bring it back to camp.

Some of the hunters were from New Jersey. They led us to believe they were part of a mafia organization. They each wore side arms and kept to themselves. They stayed at camp while I brought down the elk.

The elk was quartered and loaded onto my pack mules. I started down the trail. About a mile from camp, the pack on Maude started to slip. It was heavy, and I just couldn't get it to stay in place.

I tied the mules and unpacked their loads. Then I rode my horse down to the camp, looking for help. The two New Jersey hunters said they would help me repack the load.

Maude was like many mules in that she had a peculiarity. If you put a pack on her, it had better be hooked the first time. If it slipped down, she would always kick it.

I was on the opposite side of Maude from my helpers. I told them to boost the pannier up and be sure to hang onto it until I got it fastened.

The hunters were afraid of Maude; they didn't trust her. They boosted the pannier. Once they had it on top of her, they let go and backed away before I had an opportunity to hook it. Before it hit the ground, Maude kicked the pannier twice.

I thought she might have kicked the hunters, so I rushed around to see for sure what had happened. They were standing there in awe.

"She kicked that thing twice before it hit the ground!" they exclaimed.

"You can be thankful it wasn't *you* she kicked," I told them.

We still had to load Maude. It took quite of bit of convincing to get the men to help me again.

After that, these two hunters did a bit more mingling with us.

ANOTHER HUNTING STORY

One time, Mr. Wheeler had me pack out an elk that had been shot on a steep grade. It had been rolled into a stand of pines, where the animal was quartered.

He took me to the spot. After helping me load the elk, he and the other hunters left and went around the steep hill. I had left my saddle horse atop the grade. The grade was steep, but Maude started right up it. She and Sarah could walk up it faster than I could. Rather than be left behind, I took hold of Maude's lead rope. She bowed her neck and pulled me along. Sarah, of course, would just follow Maude anywhere.

ROXIE AND ROSIE

I have many more mule stories I could tell. But now it is time to share a draft horse story. Jackie and Julie may have been the best mares I ever owned, but Roxie was especially dear to my heart.

For years, I furnished the horses at the annual Orange City Tulip Festival and other events. You must have really well-trained horses for things like the Tulip Festival, because they are going to be around many people. You don't know what people are going to do to the horses. Some might be well-meaning and just not animal smart; others like to cause trouble.

One year, we brought two teams to town to pull two replica trolleys during the festival. People would ride the trolleys and listen to a speaker give a brief history of Orange City. The tours began at nine o'clock in the morning and paused during the parade festivities. Once the parade was over, the tours continued for another two hours. This went on for the three days of the festival.

It was during one of these morning tours that I noticed a group of young people standing on the corner by the bank, across from the park.

These young people thought it was funny to scare the horses. When we were almost to the area where we loaded people, the group would run out into the street, kicking a ball. It would frighten both my team and the other nearby team. The horses would go sideways, clear over to the curb on the other side of the street. With each trip, the teams became harder to control.

I saw a policeman and I asked him to ride along next to me, so I could show him what was happening. When the group did it again, he was able to see firsthand what I was talking about.

The policeman told the group they had to stay on the sidewalk or go elsewhere. If they scared the horses again, they would be escorted out of town. These young people stayed there, glaring at us each time we came by. But thankfully they didn't bother the horses again.

After the parade, the streets were filled with people. As we passed the courthouse during the next tour, I noticed there was a man in front of my team, waving his hands at my horses' faces and trying to scare them.

I always had an extra man riding along, just in case something went wrong. He told me the young man waving his hands had been with the bunch that morning.

There were so many people around, we were barely moving. The horses were doing real good. The young man who had been waving his hands disappeared.

Or so I thought.

Rosie, the right-hand horse, took a sudden, violent lunge forward then backward. I started yelling, *"Whoa."* On the left, Roxie absolutely froze, while her teammate gyrated and jumped all over. Rosie broke the strap to the neck yoke, then kicked the tugs off the tree.

The only thing I had to control Rosie with was the lines. The horseman I had with me jumped off. A couple other livestock men in the immediate crowd also came to my aid. The three of them got Rosie under control. If Roxie would have panicked, the team would have taken the wagon down through a packed crowd of people, and who knows what the damage would have been.

In the meantime, the crowd of people on the right-hand side were yelling, "He shot your horse! He shot your horse!".

It was determined that this fellow had an air pistol. He stuck it down by Rosie's belly. The pellet did not go through her skin, but it caused swelling and terrified her.

The young man was no longer in sight. We never did know who he was, only that he had been with the group scaring the horses in the morning.

This incident reinforced to me that you must have well-trained animals when you take them out in public. When you say, *"Whoa,"* they must freeze in their tracks.

Rosie couldn't have helped her reaction. Roxie is the one who obeyed and saved us from a tragedy. So you can see why she will always have a special place in my heart.

I had to take the team off the trolley because Rosie was so nervous. She couldn't work right, and I was afraid she would run. It took a year for her to get over this incident. Any unexpected noise at her side would make her jump.

TEACHING ART SCHOOL

In the late 1980s and into the 1990s, I was one of the instructors at a series of wildlife art classes offered by well-known artists Jack and Jessica (Zemsky) Hines. The classes were held at a Methodist church camp, in a beautiful area north of Yellowstone Park and south of Big Timber, Montana. Each class had twenty to thirty students. My focus was helping the students portray everything accurately, as it appears in nature. I instructed them on wildlife anatomy and good scale, as well as the proper use of light in their paintings.

COLLECTING AND STORYTELLING

I learned how to tell stories through my horse clinics. Before that, I had never spoken much in front of people. But when I did the horse clinics, I had to speak all day.

When it became apparent I was not only a collector of Civil War artifacts but also a historian, I was asked to speak at meetings, at schools, and at Northwestern College. One of my last presentations was recorded on a CD.

Mary Virginia and I enjoyed collecting, whether it be clocks, sleigh bells, glassware, furniture, horse-drawn machinery, or Native American artifacts. We saved it all, along with as much of the history of each item as we could gather.

Mary studied glassware by reading and visiting with knowledgeable people. She enjoyed going to auctions and antique stores. Wrangling for the best price was part of the fun.

Sometimes we found items while on farm calls. For example, Mary once went with me on a call to a client who had been with us for many years. She saw an unusual weathervane on top of their barn.

"Boy, would I ever like to have that weathervane," she said.

"I will just get a ladder and get it for you," I joked.

Later, when I was back on the farm, I told the farmer my wife admired the weathervane.

He got it down and gave it to me.

RABBIT WRENCH

Another time comes to mind when I noticed an interesting antique while on a call.

Through my horse work, I became friends with an elderly couple in Nebraska. His hobby was training light driving horses to be used on buggies and carts.

Once, when I went down there to do some work for him, they asked me to stay for dinner. As I sat in the kitchen, I noticed a framed wrench hanging on the wall in the kitchen.

We used to call this type of tool a "monkey wrench"; it was very common on farms. Everyone had one outside in their shop, but rarely in their house—especially not framed and hanging on the kitchen wall.

Upon inquiry, the wife laughed.

"That's what kept us alive during the Depression," she said. "We were living on a farm in Kansas and practically starved to death. My husband would take the old wrench along when he went hunting. If he was able to get within twenty-five to thirty feet of a jack rabbit, he would throw that wrench at it and we would have jack rabbit for supper. He was deadly with it."

I can remember him sitting at the table as she told me this story. He laughed and said, "She's right. That old wrench kept us from starving during those dry years in Kansas."

I didn't get an antique on this trip...but I did get a good story to add to my collection.

Bob Bonnecroy, Abe Schiebout, Gerrit Hulstein, and I (far left) were an authentically dressed, equipped, and mounted Union Army cavalry unit. We participated in many parades and events for several years.

Photo courtesy of the Brent and Mary Hulstein collection.

I have given many talks on the Civil War, brought alive by authentic artifacts.

Hunting was something I enjoyed doing. In 1969, it was my privilege to spend one month hunting with indigenous Canadians for their winter supply of meat. We were flown into the Mackenzie Mountains in northern Canada, where the Bonnet Plume River begins.

An advertisement for the Old Time Threshing Bee we participated in for many years at Stub Johnson's farm near Spencer, Iowa.

Santa Claus (Stub Johnson of Spencer) and I visited several towns during the Christmas season to give children rides and a treat. The horses pictured, Donna and Dot, were a feisty team.

CHAPTER TWENTY-EIGHT

My Rock of Gibraltar

One day, Mary Virginia and I received a letter informing us we had earned a substantial sum of money. Years before, she had invested in a business. She had never told me and had almost forgotten about it herself.

The business had grown manifold and recently been sold to another company for a sizeable amount of money. This letter told us a check for our share of the stock would soon be coming our way. It struck me that this windfall was due to Mary's thriftiness. Because she lived frugally, she had money to invest when the opportunity arose.

After dinner the next day, I left to go to the elevator in Hospers. While I was gone, Mary began experiencing severe pain. An aneurysm near her heart had begun leaking. At the time, we did not know she had this aneurysm. She had been checked for aneurysms in the abdomen area, but her chest was never examined.

By one o'clock in the afternoon, she was on her way to a larger hospital to undergo surgery.

Mary never fully recovered from the aneurysm and surgery. I completely quit practicing—quit everything, including my horse work—and stayed home with her. Later, when she was at the Prairie

Ridge Care Facility, I stayed with her every day. I would go in at 6:30 a.m. and stay until 9:00 p.m. If I had to be gone for a little while, I had someone stay with her.

Mary passed away on August 28, 2014.

I could never have accomplished what I did without Mary Virginia. Her life as the wife of a professional man was not always rosy. She had plenty of problems to face, a business to help run, and a family to raise. But she had the tenacity of a bulldog. She could always see the good in any situation—the bright side of things. She was the best partner I could have had.

She was my Rock of Gibraltar.

Mary by my side during one of my hospital stays.

EPILOGUE

Something to Think About

During my career, the hours I spent on the road gave me time to think and reflect on my life. There were a lot of things that bothered me. I got to wondering about why certain things had happened or turned out the way they did.

First, my thoughts would take me way back to when I was young boy, riding along with Dr. Roach. I watched him as he worked. What I saw was so often in my head, I knew that I wanted to be a veterinarian.

But when it was time for me to go to college, there was little money available. My dad said, "I don't know how we will get you through school. But if you want to go, we will help as much as we can".

I was only sixteen when I graduated from high school, too young to be drafted or join the service. So, off to college I went. And somehow, I did make it through.

The Depression had just ended. The economy was picking up due to the war effort. People had jobs, so it was somewhat easier to earn money to pay for tuition and books. Things just fell into place for me.

Then I would remember how and when I met my wife. Before that day at the paint shop, I would not have had the time or the finances for a girlfriend. I still didn't have much money when we met, but my college education was almost complete.

A job offering took me to Orange City. Even though we had only known each other a few weeks, Mary came with me on a day trip to look at the town. A year later, I married Mary Virginia and we began our life together. We joined the American Reformed Church, where our friends went. Life was good, and our family increased to five.

By 1960, my practice was going well. Dr. Fisher and I had to take in two other practitioners to get the work done. The big practice—and everything else—I had always wished for was now a reality.

That is what bothered me. It seemed I was getting everything I had prayed for, and I wondered why. I certainly knew I was not a perfect man. Why was I so blessed?

What's more, I seldom drove through the intersection north of town, where my first bad car accident occurred, without remembering that day. Two elderly people had died, and David would have too if he had been along. Mary Virginia had wanted to send him with me, and I rarely turned down her requests. But that day, I did. I have no idea why.

The Reverend Dr. Henry Colenbrander visited and prayed with me each day at the hospital after the accident, even though I wasn't a member of his congregation. When we were talking, I told him I wondered why I was spared. I also told him about all the times I could have—maybe *should have* is the right phrase—died when I was a child. The runaway horses that jumped over me. The firecracker incident.

He said to me, "The Lord has saved you to do some good thing."

"Maybe that good thing is just to raise my family and be a good veterinarian," I replied.

I wasn't looking for something big to do; I just wanted to live my ordinary life. But I still wondered why I had been spared, and why it seemed I'd gotten everything I'd prayed for.

Things started to become clear to me when I got a call from a client near Middleburg. A cow had gotten into a hog feeder and eaten all she could. She was now very ill.

The farmer wasn't able to be there, but he said the cow would be in the barn. She was in really bad shape, and he told me to put her down if I didn't think she would live. If I had any instructions for the cow's care, I was to leave a note. All this was routine—just like thousands of calls I had answered before.

On my way to this farm, I again passed the corner where the accident had happened.

As they always did, memories of that day came flooding back. I remembered how my serious injuries quickly healed without any pain, how shocked the doctors were that I had eyesight, and how soon I was back to work.

My mind returned to the man's voice I'd heard in the hospital, reciting my favorite Psalm. They tell me no one had been in the room. But I know Psalm 23 was imparted to me and that I was reassured everything would be all right.

I arrived at the farm and went into the barn. The cow was lying flat on the ground, near the manger. Upon examination, I determined she was almost dead.

When an animal overeats grain and protein like this cow had, they become so intoxicated they are unable to stand and their breathing becomes very labored. If they are given an IV, their blood is black as coal. Their eyes glaze over. Their mouths are usually open, with a dark-colored—almost black—tongue protruding out. They do not react to any stimulus.

When an animal is in that shape, just a whisper away from dying, any treatment is too late.

After looking over the cow, I did a very dangerous thing. Instead of starting what I thought would be futile treatments, I went to the corner of the barn next to the manger, got down on my knees, and prayed.

"If there is anything to this," I prayed. "If there is a power looking after me that has given me all I have asked for, I would like to see this cow get on her feet."

I prayed for quite some time. There was plenty on my mind and in my thoughts. I prayed until everything was out of my system.

Then, words I will never forget drifted into my mind: *"Get up, get going."*

I stood up and turned around. There was the dairy cow, standing and chewing her cud as if nothing had ever happened.

It scared me so bad I left that little barn as fast as I could. I got in my truck and sat there for some time, digesting what had just happened.

I do believe that, in the program of our lives, we can influence our paths to a certain extent. I also believe God has a destiny for each of us, a work He wants us to do. When I prayed that day in the barn, I began to understand that God wanted me to keep excelling in my practice and treating people well. He was going to use me and my career to help people through difficult times. I didn't fully know that at the time, but I can clearly see it now. I just had to get up and get going.

Some people will not believe what I say happened. But it is true. I can plainly see that scene in the barn today, and it still shakes me up.

I kept the story quite private. Occasionally, when a good friend of mine was approaching death and their faith was wavering, I would go talk to them and tell them my story about the cow. I would encourage them to have faith, because there is someone much greater than we who is watching us. He will help with our problems, if we just ask.

Looking back, I can now see God's hand on my life, beginning with the parents He gave me. They worked hard and stressed the importance of regularly attending Sunday school and church. If there was any extra money, they spent it on their family—not on things they wanted or needed. Money was scarce, but they gave us time and love.

God also blessed me with a good wife. Mary Virginia worked in my practice, even though she could have been doing something else. She understood the demands of my work and my devotion to it. I often said to her, "If I had married a different woman, she probably would have left me by now."

You can take the whole story of my life—all that happened to me, and the people who came into my life when I needed them—and see how God was there to orchestrate everything. It wasn't luck.

That is the reason I am writing this book—to mark the fact that I believe there is no such thing as good luck. God makes things happen, and He chooses to use us, especially as we depend on Him in prayer. His plan is already in place.

I don't know how the words, "Get up, get going," came into my mind that day in the barn, but they did. No human voice gave me this command. But I never forgot it.

Get up, get going.

I listened and did as instructed. Perhaps, after all these years, the Reverend Dr. Henry Colenbrander was right.

The Lord saved me to do some good thing.

www.ingramcontent.com/pod-product-compliance
Lightning Source LLC
Chambersburg PA
CBHW050855240426
43672CB00019B/2981